A

BIBLIOGRAPHY

OF THE

LAWS OF THE MASSACHUSETTS BAY

1641–1776

BY

WORTHINGTON CHAUNCEY FORD

AND

ALBERT MATTHEWS

REPRINTED FROM

THE PUBLICATIONS

OF

The Colonial Society of Massachusetts

VOL. IV.

THE LAWBOOK EXCHANGE, LTD.
Union, New Jersey

MARTINO PUBLISHING
Mansfield Centre, Connecticut

2003

ISBN 1-58477-284-0 The Lawbook Exchange, Ltd.
ISBN 1-57898-417-3 Martino Publishing

Printed in the United States of America
on acid-free paper

A co-publication of

The Lawbook Exchange, Ltd.
33 Terminal Avenue
Clark, New Jersey 07066

Maurizio Martino Publishing
P.O. Box 373
Mansfield Centre, CT 06250

Library of Congress Cataloging-in-Publication Data

Ford, Worthington Chauncey, 1858-1941.
A bibliography of the laws of the Massachusetts Bay, 1641-1776 / by Worthington Chauncey Ford and Albert Matthews.
p. cm.
Originally published: Cambridge : Privately printed, 1907.
"Reprinted from the Publications of the Colonial Society of Massachusetts, vol. IV."
ISBN 1-58477-284-0 (Lawbook Exchange : cloth: acid-free paper) — ISBN 1-57898-417-3 (Martino Pub. : cloth: acid-free paper)
1. Law—Massachusetts—Sources—Bibliography. 2. Statutes—Massachusetts—History—Sources—Bibliography. I. Matthews, Albert, 1860-1946. II. Title.

KFM2441 2003
016.348744'022—dc21 2002034067

A
BIBLIOGRAPHY
OF THE
LAWS OF THE MASSACHUSETTS BAY
1641–1776

BY

WORTHINGTON CHAUNCEY FORD
AND
ALBERT MATTHEWS

REPRINTED FROM
THE PUBLICATIONS
OF
The Colonial Society of Massachusetts
VOL. IV.

CAMBRIDGE •
PRIVATELY PRINTED
1907

100 copies printed.

University Press:
John Wilson and Son, Cambridge, U. S. A.

NOTE.

When connected with the Boston Public Library the question frequently arose whether a particular Law could be found in official and contemporary printed form. Upon consulting the volumes of the Laws of the Colony and of the Province of the Massachusetts Bay in that Library, I was impressed by the differences which might exist in issues apparently identical; and to prepare myself to answer inquiries I began to list the separate issues. The volumes were in few instances complete, and I was obliged to extend my examination to the volumes of the Laws in the libraries of Harvard University, the Massachusetts Historical Society, and the Boston Athenæum. As the list grew the omissions were found to be many, and the missing sheets were sought in libraries outside of the State of Massachusetts. The two largest collections, those in the Lenox Library (New York Public Library) and in the Historical Society of Pennsylvania (purchased of George H. Moore), yielded some rich results, and the list reached a fair state of completeness. To enable me to check this list it became necessary to compile a Bibliography of the Journals of the House of Representatives of the Province from 1715, which appears in the present volume. Even this did not end the labor involved, for I was called away from Boston before many items had been located and described. I was fortunate in having Mr. Albert Matthews as a collaborator, and his research discovered many titles not in my list, and detected many errors and differences in the numbers I had noticed. To his labors are due those material additions and the accuracy of citations; and to his editorial care, the correctness of the text and the typographical form in which the titles are printed.

The bibliography of the Laws of the Colony has been so fully treated by William H. Whitmore as to leave little further to be said. I may, however, call attention to the discovery of a copy of the long lost and much desired compilation of 1648, the copy described being still regarded as unique. It is in the collection of Mr. E. D. Church, of Brooklyn, New York. A second item is a manuscript in the State Archives of Massachusetts, believed to be in the writing of John Cotton, and endorsed "Opinions of the Elders, 1643." Its title is "How far Moses Judicialls bind Mass." I have printed the text, and undertaken to establish its relation to the laws of the Province, in the Proceedings of the Massachusetts Historical Society, Second Series, XVI. 274–284.

To assist those who consult this Bibliography the following table of the various compilations and subsequent issues of the Laws of Massachusetts, with the number of pages the complete volume should contain, is given.

Year of publication		Number of pages in volume when complete	Described in this Bibliography on page
1699	Permanent Laws	406	30
1714	" "	430	50
1724	" "	359	61
1726	" "	789	63
1742	Temporary "	455	85
1742	Permanent "	526	87
1755	Temporary "	550	125
1759	Permanent "	679	146
1763	Temporary "	528	157

While the practice of continuing the paging of the Laws from issue to issue, or from session to session, began in 1668, it did not become so established as to be useful till after the compilation of 1699.

The list can still only be regarded as partial, and the compilers will welcome additional items as they may be discovered.

WORTHINGTON CHAUNCEY FORD.

DECEMBER, 1907.

BIBLIOGRAPHY

OF THE

LAWS OF THE MASSACHUSETTS BAY.

1641–1776.

Key to Abbreviations.

A = Boston Athenæum.
B = Boston Public Library.
C = Library of Congress.
H = Harvard College Library.
H^L = Harvard Law School Library.[1]
J = John Carter Brown Library, Providence.
L = Lenox (New York Public) Library.
M = Massachusetts Historical Society.
N = New York Historical Society.
P = Historical Society of Pennsylvania.
S = Massachusetts State Library or Secretary's Office.
W = American Antiquarian Society, Worcester.
X = The Colonial Laws of Massachusetts, Reprinted from the Edition of 1660, with the Supplements to 1672, edited by William H. Whitmore, Boston, 1889.
Z = The Colonial Laws of Massachusetts, Reprinted from the Edition of 1672, with the Supplements through 1686, edited by William H. Whitmore, Boston, 1887.

[1] Only those items in the Harvard Law School Library are noted in this Bibliography which are not in the Harvard College Library, or which differ from the latter.

BIBLIOGRAPHY

OF THE

LAWS OF THE MASSACHUSETTS BAY.

1641–1776.

1641.

An | Abstract | or the | Lawes | of New England, | As they are novv established. | [Cut.]

London, | Printed for F. Coules, and W. Ley at Paules Chain,| 1641.

Collation: Title, 1 leaf; Text, pp. 1–15; Table, pp. (2).
Sq. 4to. B. H. J. L.

The title reads, " An | Abstract | or the | Lawes | of New England; " but the caption on p. 1 reads, " An Abstract | Of the Lavves of Nevv England."

1648.

The | Book Of General | Lauues And Libertyes | Concerning the Inhabitants of the Massachusetts | Collected out of the Records of the General Court | for the Several Years wherein they were made | and Established, | and now revised by the same Court and disposed into an Alphabetical order | and published by the same Authoritie in the General Court | held at Boston the fourteenth of the | first month Anno | 1647.| VVhosoever therefore resisteth the power, resisteth the ordinance of God, | and they that resist receive to themselves damnation. Romanes 13. 2. | [Ornament.]

Cambridge. | Printed according to Order of the General Court. | 1648. | And are to be solde at the shop of Hezekiah Usher | in Boston.

Collation: Title, 1 leaf; Preface, pp. iii, iv; Text, pp. 1–55; "Presidents and Forms of things frequently asked," pp. 55–59 [1]; [Table of contents, pp. (2) ?].

See an article by Luther S. Livingston on this compilation, printed in the Nation, 5 July, 1906 (lxxxiii. 7, 8). The copy described is believed to be unique.

1649.

An Act | For the promoting and propagating the | Gospel | of | Jesus Christ | in | New England. | [Seal of the Commonwealth.] | Die Veneris, 27 Julii, 1649. | Ordered by the Commons assembled in Parliament, That this | Act be forthwith printed and published. | Hen: Scobell, Cleric. Parliament'. | [Vignette.]

London, Printed for Edward Husband, Printer to the Parliament, of England, | and are to be sold at his Shop in Fleetstreet, at the Sign of the Golden- | Dragon, near the Inner-Temple, 1649.

Collation: Title, 1 leaf; Text, pp. 407–412. H. J. L.

1655.

An | Abstract | of | Laws and Government. | Wherein as in a Mirrour may be seen | the wisdome & perfection of the Government of | Christs Kingdome. | Accomodable to any State or form of | Government in the world, that is not Antichri- | stian or Tyrannicall. | Collected and digested into the ensuing Method, by | that Godly, Grave, and Judicious Divine, Mr. John | Cotton, of Boston in New-England, in his Life-time, | and presented to the generall Court of the Massachusets. | And now published after his death, by | William Aspinwall. | Isa. 33. 22. Jehovah is our Judge, Jehovah is our Law-giver, Je- | hovah is our King, he will save us.

London, | Printed by M. S. for Livewel Chapman, and are to be sold | at the Crown in Popes-head Alley, 1655.

Collation: Title, 1 leaf; To the Reader, pp. (5); Abstract, pp. 1-35 [1]; An Analysis of Lawes and Government accommodated to New-England, 1 p.; Errata, 1 p. B. H. L.

1660.

The | Book of the General | Lavves and Libertyes | concerning the Inhabitants of the | Massachusets, collected out of the Records of | the General Covrt, for the several years | Wherein they were made and | Established. | And | Now Revised by the same Court, and disposed into an | Alphabetical order, and published by the same | Authority in the General Court holden | at Boston, in May | 1649. VVhosoever therefore resisteth the Power, resisteth the Ordinance of God, | and they that resist, receive to themselves damnation. Rom: 13. 2.

Cambridge, | Printed according to Order of the General Covrt. | 1660.

Collation: Title, 1 leaf; Address "To our beloved Brethren and Neighbours," 1 leaf; Laws, pp. 1–88; Table pp. (8). Folio. A. H[L]. L. M. P. S. W. X.

The Harvard Law School Library copy lacks Title. The Massachusetts Historical Society has two copies, both imperfect. The American Antiquarian Society's copy, which belonged to Edward Rawson, is slightly torn.

1663.

Severall | Lavvs and Orders | Made at severall | General Courts | in the Years 1661. 1662. 1663. | Printed and Published by Order of the General Court held at Boston | the 20th of October, 1663. | By Edward Rawson Secr'.

Collation: No Title; Text, pp. 1–7 [1]. H[L]. M. W. X.

1664.

Several | Lavvs and Orders | Made at Severall | General Courts | in the Years 1661. 1662. 1664. | Printed and Published by Order of the General Court held at Boston the 19th of October, 1664. | By Edward Rawson Secr.

Collation: No title; Text, pp. 1–4. M. S. W. X.

The Massachusetts Historical Society's copy is slightly imperfect.

1665.

Several | Lavvs and Orders | Made at the | General Courts | in | May 3. August 1. & October 11. 1665. | Printed and Published by Order of the General Court held at Boston | the 11th of October, 1665. By Edward Rawson, Secr'.

Collation: No title; Text, pp. 1–3 [1]. HL. W. X.

1666.

Severall | Lavvs and Orders | Made at the | General Court | Held at Boston, the 23d of May, 1666. And on the | 11th of October following. | Printed and Published by Order of the General Court, the said 11th of | October, 1666. | By Edward Rawson Secr.

Collation: No title; Text, pp. 1–3 [1]. HL. W. X.

1668.

Several | Lavvs and Orders | Made at the | General Court | of | Election. | Held at Boston in | New-England | the 29th. of April 1668. | Printed and Published by their Order. | Edward Rawson Secr.

Collation: No title; Text, pp. 1–9[1]. HL. W. X.

The Harvard Law School Library copy lacks pp. 1, 2, 8, 9. Pages 8, 9, are inside pages facing one another. They contain the action of the General Court on the three "Obstinate and Turbulent Anabaptists," Thomas Gold, William Turner, and John Farnham, Senior.

1668.

Several | Lavvs | and | Orders | Made at the | General Court, | Held at Boston in New-England, | October 14. 1668.

| Printed and Published by their Order. | Edward Rawson Secr.

Cambridge Printed in the Year, 1668.

Collation: Title, 1 leaf; Text, pp. 9–20. HL. W. X.

The American Antiquarian Society's copy lacks pp. 19, 20, and has pp. 17, 18, torn.

1669.

Several | Laws and Orders | Made at the | Generall Court of Election | Held at Boston, May 19th 1669. | And Printed and Published by their Order, June 4. 1669. | Edw. Rawson, Secret'.

Collation: No title; pp. 21–27 [1]. HL. X.

1672.

The | Book of the General | Laws | Of the Inhabitants of the Jurisdiction of | New-Plimouth; | Collected out of the Records of the | General Court | And lately revised, and with some Emendations and Additions, Established | and Disposed into such Order as they may readily conduce to ge- | neral use and benefit, | And published by the Authority of the General Court for that | Jurisdiction, held at Plimouth, the sixth of June, | Anno Dom. 1671. | Be subject to every Ordinance of Man for the Lords sake. 1 Pet. 2. 13.

Cambridge: | Printed by Samuel Green 1672.

Collation: Title, 1 leaf; Address "To our Beloved Brethren and Neighbours," 1 leaf; Laws, pp. 1–47 [1]; List of Errata (p. 47), 3 lines; Table, pp. (8). B. HL. M.

The Harvard Law School Library copy has Title and the last leaf of Table in reprint. The Massachusetts Historical Society's copy lacks pp. 1–4.

1672.

The General | Laws | and | Liberties | of the | Massachusets | Colony: | Revised & Re-printed. | By Order of the General Court Holden at Boston, | May 15th. 1672 | Edward Rawson Secr. | Whosoever therefore resisteth the Power, resisteth the Ordinance of God, and they that resist receive to themselves Damnation. Rom. 13, 2.

Cambridge | Printed by Samuel Green, for John Usher of Boston. | 1672.

Collation: Colony Seal, 1 leaf; Title, 1 leaf; Laws, pp. 1–161[1]; "Presidents & Formes of things frequently Used," pp. 162 [163]–170 [171] [1]; Errata, nine lines on p. 170 [171]; Table, pp. (27).

A. B. C. H. J. L. M. P. S. W. Z.

One copy in the Boston Athenæum has the Colony Seal on the verso of Title. Another copy belonged to Elisha Hutchinson, the grandfather of Governor Thomas Hutchinson, and has notes in his hand. The Library of Congress copy lacks Title and pp. 1–4. The Lenox Library copy lacks the Colony Seal. The Massachusetts Historical Society has two copies, both lacking the Colony Seal. The Massachusetts State Library copy has Title torn, and lacks the Colony Seal and the last two leaves of Table.

1672.

Several Laws and Orders made at the | General Court, | Holden at Boston the 15th. of May | 1672. | And Printed by their Order. | Edward Rawson Secr.

Collation: No title; Text, pp. 1–6. A. B. C. H. J. L. S. W. Z.

1673.

Several Laws and Orders made at the | General Court, | the 8th. of October 1672 | as also | Several Laws and Orders made at the | General Courts, | holden at Boston the 7th. of May and 15th of | October, 1673. | And printed by their Order. | Edward Rawson Secr.

Collation: No title; pp. 7–12. A. B. H. J. L. M. S. W. Z.

The Massachusetts Historical Society's copy has pp. 9, 10, mutilated.

1673–74.

Orders, | Made at A | General Court | held at Boston, January the 6th. 1673. | And Printed by their Order. | Edward Rawson Secret.

Collation: No title; p. 13 [1]. A. B. Z.

1674.

Several | Laws and Orders | Made at the | General Court | Holden at Boston the twenty seventh of May | 1674. | And Printed by their Order, | Edward Rawson Secret.

Collation: No title; pp. 11 [13]–15 [1]. A. B. C. H. M. S. W. Z.

1674.

Several Laws and Orders Made at the | Second Sessions of the | General Court, | held at Boston in New England the | Seventh of October 1674 | And printed by their Order | Edward Rawson Secr.

Collation: No title; pp. 17–18 [1], printed on inside pages. A. L. M. Z.

1675.

Several | Lavvs & Orders | Made at the | General Court | Holden at Boston the twelfth of May | 1675. | And Printed by their Order, | Edward Rawson. Secrt.

Collation: No title; pp. 19–21 [1]. A. B. C. P. S. W. Z.

Some copies have "Lavvs," other copies have "Laws." The Boston Athenæum has both editions. In the American Antiquarian Society's copy, and in one of the Boston Athenæum copies, p. 19 is misnumbered 17.

1675.

[Colony Seal.] | At a | Council | Held in Boston August the thirtieth 1675.

Collation: No title; 1 leaf, unpaged. A. Z.

Order in regard to Indians. The Boston Athenæum copy is slightly torn.

1675.

Several | Laws and Orders | Made at the Sessions of the | General Court | Held at Boston the 13th of October 1675. | As also at the Sessions of Court | held at Boston, the 3d. of Novemb. | 1675. | And Printed by their Order, | Edward Rawson Secr.

Cambridge, | Printed by Samuel Green. 1675.

Collation: Title, 1 leaf; Text, pp. 25–40.

A. B. C. L. P. S. W. Z.

The Library of Congress copy and the American Antiquarian Society's copy alone have Title. Pages 29–31 contain the "Lawes & Ordinances of Warre," with the following caption:

Laws & Ordinances | of Warre, | Pas'd by the General Court of the Massachusets, | for the better Regulating their Forces and | keeping their Souldiers to their Duty, and to | prevent Prophaneness, that Iniquity may be | kept out of the Camp.

1675.

The General | Laws | and | Liberties | of the | Massachusets Colony | in | New England, | Revised and Reprinted, | By order of the General Court holden at Boston, | May 15th, 1672. | Edward Rawson, Secr. | Whosoever therefore resisteth the Power, | resisteth the Ordinance of God; and | they that resist, receive to themselves Damnation. Rom. 13. 2.

Cambridge in New-England, | Printed by Samuel Green, for John Usher of Boston, and to be sold by | Richard Chiswel, at the Rose and Crown in St. Paul's Church-yard, | London, 1675.

Collation: Title, 1 leaf; Text, pp. 1–161 [1]; "Presidents & Formes of things frequently Used," pp. 162 [163]–170 [171] [1]; Errata, ten lines on p. 170 [171]; Table, pp. (28); List of Book, 1 leaf. J. P. W.

The American Antiquarian Society's copy lacks pp. 168, 169, and has pp. 1, 2, torn.

1675–76.

[Colony Seal.] | Several | Lavvs & Orders | Made at the | General Court | Held at Boston the 21st. of February, 1675. | And Printed by their Order, | Edward Rawson, Secr't.

Collation: No title; pp. 41–43 [1]. A. B. W. Z.

1676.

[Colony Seal.] | At a | Council | Held at Boston, April the 4th. 1676.

Collation: No title; 1 leaf, unpaged. A. Z.

The Boston Athenæum copy is slightly torn.

1676.

[Colony Seal.] | Several | Laws & Orders | Made at the | General Court, | Held at Boston for Election the 3d. of | May 1676 | And Printed by their Order, | Edward Rawson Secr.

Collation: No title; pp. 45–48. A. B. S. W. Z.

The American Antiquarian Society's copy has pp. 45, 46, torn.

1676.

[Colony Seal.] | At a | General Court | Held at Boston May the 3d, 1676.

Collation: No title; 1 leaf, unpaged. A. Z.

1676.

[Colony Seal.] | At a | General Court | Held at Boston the 3d. of May | 1676.

Collation: No title; 1 leaf, unpaged. A. Z.

1677.

[Colony Seal.] | At a Court | Held at Boston in | Nevv-England | the 29th. of March, 1677

Collation: No title; 1 leaf, unpaged. A. Z.

The Boston Athenæum copy is slightly torn.

1677.

[Colony Seal.] | At a Council | Held at Boston the 9th. of April, 1677

Collation: No title; 1 leaf, unpaged. A. Z.

The Boston Athenæum copy is slightly torn.

1677.

[Colony Seal.] | Several | Lavvs & Orders | Made at the first Sessions of the | General Court | for Elections | held at Boston in New-England | May 23d. 1677. | Printed and Published by their Order, | Edward Rawson Secr't.

Collation: No title; pp. 49–55 [1]. A. B. M. S. W. Z.

The Massachusetts Historical Society's copy lacks pp. 49, 50. The Massachusetts State Library copy lacks pp. 53, 54, and has pp. 49–52 mutilated. The American Antiquarian Society's copy has pp. 49, 50, torn.

1677.

[Colony Seal.] | Several | Laws and Orders | Made at the second Sessions of the | General Court | held at Boston October. 10th. 1677. | And published by Order thereof, | Edward Rawson Secr'.

Collation: No title; pp. 57–59 [1]. A. B. M. W. Z.

The American Antiquarian Society's copy has pp. 57, 58, torn.

1677.

[Colony Seal.] | Sundry Laws | Made by the General Court Wherein the Du- | ty of Tything Men is expressed, viz.

Collation: No title; pp. 1–3 [1]. A. M. Z.

1678.

[Colony Seal.] | At a | Council | Held at Boston, March 28. 1678.

Collation: No title; 1 leaf, unpaged. A. Z.

1678.

[Colony Seal.] | Several | Laws and Orders | Made at the second Sessions of the | General Court | Held at Boston, October 2^d. 1678. | And published by their Order. | Edward Rawson Secr. |

Collation: No title; pp. 61–64. A. S. Z.

The copy in the Massachusetts State Library is mutilated.

1679.

[Colony Seal.] | Several | Laws and Orders | Made at the first Sessions of the | General Court | Held at Boston, May 28. 1679, and published by their Order. | Edward Rawson Secretary

Collation: No title; pp. 65–68. A. B. Z.

1679.

[Colony Seal.] | Several | Laws and Orders | Made at the second Sessions of the | General Court | Holden at Boston Octob. 15. 1679. and Printed by their Order, | Edward Rawson Secr.

Collation: No title; pp. 69–72. A. B. Z.

1679–80.

[Colony Seal.] | Several | Laws and Orders | made at a | General Court | Held at Boston, February the 4th. $16\frac{79}{80}$ | Edward Rawson Secretary.

Collation: No title; pp. 74, 75 [1], printed on inside pages. A. B. Z.

1680.

[Colony Seal.] | Several | Laws and Orders | Made at the first Sessions of the | General Court | for | Elections | Held at Boston, May 19. 1680. | And published by their Order; | Edward Rawson Secr'.

Collation: No title; 2 leaves, unpaged, printed on inside pages. A. B. Z.

1680.

[Colony Seal.] | Several | Lavvs and Orders | Made at the second Sessions of | The General Court | Held at Boston, Octob. 13. 1680. | And Published by their Order. | Edward | Rawson Secr'.

Collation: No title; pp. 77–79 [1]. A. B. Z.

1680–81.

[Colony Seal.] | At a Sessions of the | General Court | Held at Boston the 4th of March | 1680.

Collation: No title; 1 leaf, unpaged. A. Z.

1680–81.

[Colony Seal.] | Several | Laws and Orders | Made at a Sessions of the | General Court | Held at Boston by Adjournment from the 4th. to the 16th. | of March, 1680. and published by their Order, | Edvvard Ravvson Secr.

Collation; No title; pp. [1] 82, 83 [1]. B.

1680–82.

[Colony Seal.] | Several | Lavvs and Orders | Made at the Several | General Courts | Held in Boston in the Years 1680, 1681, | And Published by their Order: | Edward Rawson Secretary.

Collation: No title; pp. 87–92. A. B. W. Z.

The first Order is dated March 16, 1680–81, and the last February 15, 1681–82. The American Antiquarian Society's copy has a fragment only of pp. 87, 88.

1682.

[Colony Seal.] | At a | General Court | Held at Boston; May 24th. 1682.

Collation: No title; 1 leaf, unpaged. A. B. Z.

Making Pieces of Eight "currant Money of New England according to their weight in the present New-England Coyne"

1682.

[Colony Seal.] | Several | Lavvs | Made at the second Session of the | General Court | Held at Boston, October 11. 1682. | And Printed by their Order, | Edward Rawson Secr'

Collation: No title; pp. 93–96. A. B. Z.

1682.

[Colony Seal.] | An | Order | for regulating Constables Payments, | And for the Rating of Unimproved Lands; and Relating to | Troopers, Made at the second Session of the

| General Court | Held at Boston, Octob. 11. 1682. | Edward Rawson Secr'

Collation: No title; 2 leaves, unpaged, printed on inside pages. A. Z.

1683.

[Colony Seal.] | Several Lavvs | made at the | General Court | Called and Held at Boston on the seventh of February, and | Continued by Adjournment to the thirty first of March 1683. | And by their Order Printed and Published; | By Edward Rawson Secretary.

Collation: No title; pp. 97–99 [1]. A. B. W. Z.

The American Antiquarian Society's copy has pp. 97, 98, torn.

1683.

[Colony Seal.] | At a | General Court | Held at Boston May. 16. 1683.

Collation: No title; 1 leaf unpaged. A. Z.

Order relating to the rating of cattle.

1683.

[Colony Seal.] | Several | Laws | made at the second Sessions of the | General Court | Held at Boston October 10. 1683. And | Published by their Order: | Edward Rawson Secr.

Collation: No title; pp. [1] 98, 99 [1] A. B. Z.

They are printed on the inside pages of two leaves, and should have been paged 102, 103, in regular sequence. The American Antiquarian Society's copy has p. 98 torn.

1683.

[Colony Seal.] | At a Special | General Court | Held at Boston Novemb. 7. 1683.

Collation: No title; 1 leaf, unpaged. A. Z.

An Order relating to building in Boston.

1683–84.

[Colony Seal.] | At a | General Court | on Adjournment, Held at Boston | Feb. 13 168¾

Collation: No title; 1 leaf, unpaged. A. Z.

An Order relating to building in Boston.

1684.

[Colony Seal.] | Several | Laws and Orders | Made by the | General Court, | Held at Boston the 7th. of May, 1684.

Collation: No title; pp. [1] 100, 101 [1]. A. W. Z.

They are printed on the inside pages of two leaves. The American Antiquarian Society's copy is mutilated.

1684.

[Colony Seal.] | At a | General Court | Called by the Honourable Governour on His Receipt of His | Majesties Letter, to sit in Boston, July the 9th. 1684. When | they Sate there was Made and Passed the Law and Order fol- | lowing; And by their Order Printed: | By the Court Edward Rawson Secr'.

Collation: No title; pp. 103–105 [1]. A. B. Z.

1684.

[Colony Seal.] | Several | Lavvs | made at the | General Court | Called to Sit, and Held at Boston, Sept. 10th. 1684. | And Published by their Order, | Edward Rawson Secr.

Collation: No title; pp. 107–109 [1]. A. W. Z.

The American Antiquarian Society's copy is mutilated.

1684.

[Colony Seal.] | Several | Orders and Laws | Made at the Second Sessions of the | General Court | Held at Boston, Octob: 15th. 1684. | And Printed by their | Order: | Edward Rawson Secr'.

Collation: No title; pp. 110, 111, on two leaves, printed on inside pages. A. P. W. Z.

The American Antiquarian Society's copy is mutilated.

1684–85.

[Colony Seal.] | At a | General Court | Held at Boston, January 28. 1684.

Collation: No title; 1 leaf, unpaged. A. Z.

1684–85.

[Colony Seal.] | The Governour and Company | Of the Massachusets Bay in New-England. | at a | General Court | Held at Boston, by Adjournment from the 28th of January | to the 18th of March, 1684.

Collation: No title; 1 leaf, unpaged. B. Z.

1685.

[Colony Seal.] | By the | Governour and Council | Assembled at Boston the 2d. of April, 1685. | To all His Majesties Subjects within the Government of the | Massachusets Colony.

Collation: No title; 1 leaf, unpaged. A. Z.

1685.

[Colony Seal.] | Several | Laws and Orders | made by the | Governour and Company | Of the Massachusets Bay in New-England | at the | General Court | Held at Boston, May 27th 1685. | As also at a General Court Held at Boston on | the 14th of October, 1685. | And Printed by Order, | Edward Rawson Secretary.

Collation: No title; pp. 121–123 [1]. A. Z.

1685

The Book of the General | Laws | of the Inhabitants of the | Jurisdiction of | New-Plimouth, | Collected out of the Records of the | General Court, | and lately Revised: | And with some Emendations and Additions Established and Disposed into such | Order as they may readily Conduce to General Use and Benefit. | And by the Order and Authority of the General Court of New-Plimouth Held | at Plimouth, June 2d. Anno Dom. 1685. Reprinted and Published; | Nathaniel Clerk Secrt'. | [Cut of the Colonial Arms.] Be subject to every Ordinance of Man for the Lords sake, 1 Pet. 2. 13.

Boston in New-England: | Printed by Samuel Green. 1685.

Collation: Title, 1 leaf; "A Preface," pp. 4; Laws, pp. 1–75 [1]; Table, pp. (9); List of Errata, 12 lines.

A. C. L. M.

The Boston Athenæum copy has no List of Errata. The Lenox Library has a fragment, pp. 19–22 only.

1685–86.

[Colony Seal.] | By the | Governour and Company | Of the Massachusets Bay in New-England | at a | General Court | Held at Boston, on Adjournment, Feb. 16th 1685.

Collation: No title; pp. 125, 126. A. Z.

1689.

A Copy | of the | Kings Majesties | Charter, | For Incorporating the Company of the | Massachusetts Bay in New-England in America. | Granted in the fourth Year of his Highness Reign of England, Scotland, | France and Ireland, Anno Dom. 1628. | [Colony Seal.]

Boston in New-England, | Printed by S. Green, for Benj. Harris at the London Coffee House | near the Town-House in Boston. 1689.

Collation: Title, 1 leaf; Charter, pp. 1–26. A. M.

The Boston Athenæum copy lacks Title and is eaten by book-worms.

1692.

The | Charter | Granted by their Majesties | King William | and | Queen Mary, | to the | Inhabitants | of the | Province | of the | Massachusets-Bay, | in | New-England.

London: | Printed in the Year 1692

Collation: Title, 1 leaf; Text, pp. 1–13 [1]. B. L.

1692.

The | Charter | Granted by their Majesties | King William | And | Queen Mary, | to the | Inhabitants | of the | Province | of the | Massachusetts-Bay, | in | New-England.

Printed at London, and Re=Printed at Boston, in New-England, By | Benjamin Harris, Over-against the Old-Meeting-House. 1692.

Collation: Title, 1 leaf; Text, pp. 1–13 [1]. A. W.

1692.

Several | Acts | and | Laws | Passed by the Great and General Court or | Assembly of Their Majesties Province | of the Massachusetts-Bay, in | New England. | Convened and Held at Boston, the Eighth Day of June. 1692. | Anno Regni Gulielmi, et Mariæ, Regis et Reginæ Angliæ, Scotiæ, | Franciæ, et Hiberniæ, Quarto.

Boston, | Printed by Benjamin Harris, Printer to His Excellency, | the Governour and Council. 1692.

Collation: Title, 1 leaf; Text, pp. 1–16.
A. B. H^L. L. P. W.

The Harvard Law School Library copy lacks Title. The Lenox Library copy lacks Title, but has a duplicate of pp. 11–16, with variations, purchased at the Brinley sale.

1692.

Acts | and Laws, | Passed by the Great and General Court or Assembly of Their Majesties Pro- | vince of the Mass-| achusets-Bay, in | New-England. | Begun at Boston, the Eighth Day of June, 1692. And Con- | tinued by Adjournment, unto Wednesday the Twelfth | Day of October following: Being the Second Sessions. | Anno Regni Gulielmi, et Mariæ, Regis et Reginæ Angliæ, Scotiæ, | Franciæ, et Hiberniæ, Quarto.

Boston | Printed by Benjamin Harris, Printer to His Excellency, | the Governour and Council. 1692.

Collation: Authorization, 1 leaf; Title, 1 leaf; Text, pp. 1–90; Contents, 1 leaf. A. B. H^{L}. L. M. P. S. W.

The Boston Athenæum copy lacks Authorization and Contents. The Massachusetts Historical Society's copy has pp. 89, 90, torn. The Massachusetts State Library copy has Text only.

1693.

Acts | and | Laws, | Passed by the Great and General Court | or Assembly of Their Majesties Pro- | vince of the Massachusets-Bay, in | New-England. | Begun at Boston the Eighth Day of June, 1692, And Con- | tinued by several Adjournments unto Wednesday the Eighth | of February following, being the Third Sessions. | Anno Regni, Gulielmi, et Mariæ, Regis et Reginæ, Angliæ, | Scotiæ, Franciæ, et Hiberniæ Quarto, et Quinto. | [Royal Arms.]

Boston | Printed by Benjamin Harris, Printer to His Excellency | the Governour and Council, 1693.

Collation: Title, 1 leaf; Text, pp. 1–6. A. B. L. P. S. W.

1693.

An | Act | Passed by the Great and General Court | or Assembly of Their Majesties Prov- | ince of the Massachusets Bay in | New-England. | Begun at Boston the Eighth Day of June 1692, And Con- | tinued by several Adjournments unto Thursday the Second | of March following, being the Fourth Sessions. | Anno Regni, Gulielmi et Mariæ, Regis et Reginæ, Angliæ, | Scotiæ, Franciæ, et Hiberniæ Quinto. | [Royal Arms.]

Boston | Printed by Benjamin Harris, Printer to his Excellency, | the Governour and Council 1693.

Collation: Title, 1 leaf; Text, pp. 1, 2. A. B. H^{L}. L. S. W.

1693.

Acts | and | Laws, | Passed by the Great and General | Court or Assembly of Their | Majesties Province of the | Massachusetts-Bay, in | New-England. | Convened and held at Boston, the Thirty-first | Day of May. 1693. | Anno Regni Guilelmi, et Mariæ, Regis et Reginæ, Angliæ, | Scotiæ, Franciæ, et Hiberniæ, Quinto.

Boston. | Printed by Bartholomew Green, and Sold by | Samuel Phillips. 1693. |

Collation: Title, 1 leaf; Text, pp. 3–15 [1].

A. B. H^{L}. L. M. P. S.

The Boston Public Library copy lacks Title and pp. 3, 4.

1693.

Acts | and | Laws, | Passed by the Great and General | Court or Assembly of Their | Majesties Province of the | Massachusetts-Bay, in | New-England. | Begun at Boston, the Thirty-first Day of May. 1693. | And Continued by Adjournment unto Thursday the Sixth | Day of July following: Being the Second Sessions. | Anno Regni Guilielmi, et Mariæ, Regis et Reginæ, Angliæ, | Scotiæ, Franciæ, et Hiberniæ, Quinto.

Boston. | Printed by Bartholomew Green, and Sold by | Samuel Phillips. 1693.

Collation: Title, 1 leaf; Text, pp. 3, 4.

A. B. H^{L}. L. M. P. S. W.

The American Antiquarian Society's copy has Title and fragment only of Text. The Harvard Law School Library copy is mutilated.

1693.

Acts | and | Laws, | Passed by the Great and General | Court or Assembly of Their | Majesties Province of the | Massachusetts-Bay, in | New-England. | Convened and Held at Boston, the Eighth Day | of November. 1693. | Anno Regni Guilielmi, et Mariæ, Regis et Reginæ, Angliæ, | Scotiæ, Franciæ, et Hiberniæ, Quinto. | [Royal Arms.]

Boston. | Printed by Bartholomew Green, and Sold by | Samuel Phillips. 1693. |

Collation: Title, 1 leaf; Text, pp. 18–48.

A. B. H^L. L. M. P. S.

Pages 19, 20, are misnumbered 18, 19.

1694.

Acts | and | Laws, | Passed by the Great and General | Court or Assembly of Their | Majesties Province of the | Massachusetts-Bay, in | New-England. | Begun at Boston, the Eighth Day of November, 1693. And | Continued by Adjournment unto Wednesday the Fourteenth | Day of February following: Being the Second Sessions. | Anno Regni Guilielmi, et Mariæ, Regis et Reginæ, Angliæ, | Scotiæ, Franciæ, et Hiberniæ, Sexto. | [Royal Arms.]

Boston. | Printed by Bartholomew Green, and Sold by | Samuel Phillips. 1694.

Collation: Title, 1 leaf; Text, pp. 49–60.

A. B. H^L. L. M. P. S.

1694.

Acts | and | Laws, | Passed by the Great and General | Court or Assembly of Their | Majesties Province of the | Massachusetts-Bay, in | New-England. | Convened and Held at Boston, on Wednesday the | Thirtieth of May. 1694. | Anno Regni Guilielmi, et Mariæ, Regis et Reginæ, Angliæ, | Scotiæ, Franciæ, et Hiberniæ, Sexto. | [Royal arms.]

Boston. | Printed by Bartholomew Green, Printer to His Excellency, | the Governour and Council. 1694.

Collation: Title, 1 leaf, Text, pp. 61–76. A. B. L. M. S. W.

The American Antiquarian Society's copy lacks pp. 67–76, and has Title torn.

1694.

Acts | and | Laws, | Passed by the Great and General | Court or Assembly of Their | Majesties Province of the | Massachusetts-Bay, in | New England. | Begun at Boston, the Thirtieth Day of May, 1694. And | Continued by Adjournment unto Wednesday the Fifth | Day of September following: Being the Second Sessions. | Anno Regni Guilielmi, et Mariæ, Regis et Reginæ, | Angliæ, Scotiæ, Franciæ, et Hiberniæ, Sexto. | [Royal Arms.]

Boston. | Printed by Bartholomew Green, Printer to His Excellency, | the Governour and Council. 1694.

Collation: Title, 1 leaf; Text, pp. 77–85 [1].

A. B. L. M. S.

The Boston Public Library copy lacks p. 85. The Massachusetts Historical Society's copy has pp. 79, 80, torn.

1694.

Acts | and | Laws, | Passed by the Great and General | Court or Assembly of Their | Majesties Province of the | Massachusetts-Bay, in | New-England. | Begun at Boston, the Thirtieth Day of May, 1694. And | Continued by Adjournments unto Tuesday the Sixteenth | Day of October following: Being the Third Sessions. | Anno Regni Guilielmi, et Mariæ, Regis et Reginæ, | Angliæ, Scotiæ, Franciæ, et Hiberniæ, Sexto. | [Royal Arms.]

Boston. | Printed by Bartholomew Green, Printer to His Excellency, | the Governour and Council. 1694.

Collation: Title, 1 leaf; Text, pp. 87–95 [1].

A. B. L. M. S.

The Massachusetts Historical Society's copy has pp. 87, 88, torn.

1695.

Acts | and | Laws | Passed by the Great and General | Court or Assembly of Their | Majesties Province of the |

Massachusetts-Bay in | New-England. | Begun at Boston the Thirtieth Day of May, 1694. And | Continued by several Adjournments unto Wednesday the Twenty- | Seventh Day of February following: Being the Fourth Sessions. | Anno Regni Guilielmi, et Mariæ, Regis et Reginæ, | Angliæ, Scotiæ, Franciæ, et Hiberniæ, Septimo. | [Royal Arms.]

Boston. | Printed by Bartholomew Green, Printer to His Excellency, | the Governour and Council. 1695.

Collation: Title, 1 leaf; Text, pp. 97–114. A. B. L. M. S.

The Boston Public Library copy is torn. The Massachusetts Historical Society's copy lacks Title and pp. 97, 98, 109–114, and has pp. 101, 102, torn.

1695.

Acts | and | Laws, | Passed by the Great and General | Court or Assembly of His | Majesties Province of the | Massachusetts-Bay, in | New-England. | Begun and Held at Boston, on Wednesday the | Twenty-ninth of May. 1695. | Anno Regni Guilielmi, Tertii, Angliæ, Scotiæ, | Franciæ, et Hiberniæ, Regis, Septimo. | [Royal Arms.]

Boston. | Printed by Bartholomew Green, Printer to the Governour | and Council. 1695.

Collation: Title, 1 leaf; Text, pp. 117–134. A. B. L. M. S.

The Massachusetts State Library copy has Title torn.

1695.

Acts | and | Laws, | Passed by the Great and General Court | or Assembly of His Majesties Province | of the Massachusetts-Bay, in | New-England. | Begun at Boston the Twenty-ninth Day of May, 1695. | and continued by Adjournment until Wednesday the | Fourteenth of August following. | Anno Regni Guilielmi, Tertii, Angliæ, Scotiæ, | Franciæ, et Hiberniæ, Regis, Septimo. | [Royal Arms.]

Boston. | Printed by Bartholomew Green and John Allen, Printers | to the Governour and Council. 1695.

Collation: Title, 1 leaf; Text, pp. 137, 138. A. B. L. S.

1695.

Acts | and | Laws, | Passed by the Great and General Court | or Assembly of His Majesties Province | of the Massachusetts-Bay, in | New-England. | Begun at Boston the Twenty-ninth Day of May, 1695. | and continued by several Adjournments until Wednesday | the Twentieth of November following. | Anno Regni Guilielmi Tertii Angliæ, Scotiæ, | Franciæ, et Hiberniæ, Regis, Septimo. | [Royal Arms.]

Boston. | Printed by Bartholomew Green and John Allen, Printers | to the Governour and Council. 1695.

Collation: Title, 1 leaf; Text, pp. 141–150.
A. B. L. M. P. S.

1696.

[Royal Arms.] | At the Parliament begun at Westminster the Two and twentieth Day of | November Anno Dom. 1695. In the Seventh Year of the Reign of our | Sovereign Lord William the Third, by the Grace of God, of England, | Scotland, France and Ireland, King, Defender of the Faith, &c.

London, Printed by Charles Bill, and the Executrix of Thomas Newcomb, | deceas'd; Printers to the Kings most Excellent Majesty. Reprinted at | Boston in New England by Bartholomew Green & John Allen, | Printers to the Governour & Council. 1696.

Collation: No title; pp. 1–8. W.

An Act for Preventing Frauds, and Regulating Abuses in the Plantation Trade.

1696.

Acts | and | Laws, | Passed by the Great and General Court | or Assembly of His Majesties Province | of the Massachusetts-Bay, in | New-England. | Begun & Held at Boston the Twenty-ninth Day of May, 1695. | and continued by several Adjournments until Wednesday | the Twenty-sixth of February following. | Anno Regni Guilielmi Tertii, Angliæ, Scotiæ, | Franciæ, et Hiberniæ, Regis, Octavo. | [Royal Arms.]

Boston. | Printed by Bartholomew Green, and John Allen, Printers | to the Governour and Council. 1696.

Collation: Title, 1 leaf; Text, pp. 153–157 [1].

A. B. L. M. S.

1696.

Acts | and | Laws, | Passed by the Great and General Court | or Assembly of His Majesties Province | of the Massachusetts-Bay, in | New-England. | Begun and Held at Boston on Wednesday the | Twenty-seventh of May, 1696. | Anno Regni Guilielmi Tertii, Angliæ, Scotiæ, | Franciæ, et Hiberniæ, Regis, Octavo. | [Royal Arms.]

Boston. | Printed by Bartholomew Green, and John Allen, Printers | to the Governour and Council. 1696.

Collation: Title, 1 leaf; Text, pp. 159–175 [1].

A. B. L. M. S.

The Boston Public Library copy lacks Title and pp. 173–175. The Massachusetts State Library copy lacks pp. 171–174.

1696.

[Royal Arms.] Acts & Laws, | Passed by the Great & General Court or | Assembly of His Majesties Province of | the Massachusetts-Bay, in New-England. | Begun at Boston the Twenty-seventh Day of May, 1696. | and continued by Adjournment until Wednesday the | Sixteenth of September following. | Anno Regni Guilielmi Tertii, Angliæ, Scotiæ, Franciæ, et | Hiberniæ, Regis, Octavo.

Boston. | Printed by Bartholomew Green, and John Allen Printers to | the Governour and Council. 1696.

Collation: No title; Text, pp. 177–180. A. L. M.

1696.

Acts | and | Laws, | Passed by the Great and General Court | or Assembly of His Majesties Province | of the Massachusetts-Bay, in | New England. | Begun at Boston the Twenty-seventh of May, 1696. | and continued by several Adjournments until Wednesday | the Eighteenth of November following. | Anno Regni Guilielmi Tertii, Angliæ, Scotiæ, | Franciæ, et Hiberniæ, Regis, Octavo. | [Royal Arms.]

Boston. | Printed by Bartholomew Green, and John Allen, Printers | to the Governour and Council. 1696.

Collation: Title, 1 leaf; Text, pp. 181–197 [1]. A. L. M. S.

The Lenox Library copy lacks pp. 195–197. The Massachusetts State Library copy lacks pp. 189–197.

1697.

Acts | and | Laws, | Passed by the Great and General Court | or Assembly of His Majesties Province | of the Massachusetts-Bay, in | New-England. | Begun and Held at Boston on Wednesday the | Twenty-sixth of May, 1697. | Anno Regni Guilielmi Tertii, Angliæ, Scotiæ, | Franciæ, et Hiberniæ, Regis, Nono. | [Royal Arms.]

Boston. | Printed by Bartholomew Green, and John Allen, Printers | to the Governour and Council, 1697.

Collation: Title, 1 leaf; Text, pp. 199–228. M. W.

The American Antiquarian Society's copy lacks Title.

1697.

Acts | and Laws, | Passed by the Great and General Court | or Assembly of His Majesties Province | of the

Massachusetts-Bay, in | New-England. | Begun and Held at Boston the Twenty-sixth of May, 1697. | and continued by Several Prorogations until Wednesday the | Thirteenth of October following: being the Third Session. | Anno Regni Guilielmi Tertii, Angliæ, Scotiæ, | Franciæ, et Hiberniæ, Regis, Nono. | [Royal Arms.]

Boston. | Printed by Bartholomew Green, and John Allen, Printers | to the Governour and Council. 1697.

Collation: Title, 1 leaf; Text, pp. 229–247 [1]. M.

1697.

Copy of the Orders for Repealing of | several Acts. | At the | Court at Whitehall. | The 22d. Day of August, 1695.

Colophon: Boston in New England. | Printed by Order of the Honourable the Lieutenant Governour | and Council; by Bartholomew Green, and John Allen. | 1697.

Collation: No title; pp. 3. L. W.

1698.

Acts | and | Laws, | Passed by the Great and General Court | or Assembly of His Majesties Province | of the Massachusetts-Bay, in | New-England. | Begun and Held at Boston on Wednesday, the | Twenty-fifth of May, 1698. | Anno Regni Guilielmi Tertii, Angliæ, Scotiæ, | Franciæ, et Hiberniæ, Regis, Decimo. | [Royal Arms.]

Boston. | Printed by Bartholomew Green, and John Allen, Printers to the | Governour and Council. 1698.

Collation: Title, 1 leaf; Text, pp. 251–300. M. P. W.

The American Antiquarian Society's copy lacks pp. 287–300.

1698.

Acts | and | Laws, | Passed by the Great and General Court | or Assembly of His Majesties Province | of the Massachusetts-Bay, in | New-England. | Begun and Held at Boston the Twenty-fifth Day of May, 1698. | and continued by Prorogation until Tuesday the Fifteenth | of November following: being the Second Session. | Anno Regni Guilielmi Tertii, Angliæ, Scotiæ, | Franciæ, et Hiberniæ, Regis, Decimo. | [Royal Arms.]

Boston. | Printed by Bartholomew Green, and John Allen, Printers to the | Governour and Council. 1698.

Collation: Title, 1 leaf; Text, pp. 301-321 [1]. M.

1699.

Order of their Excellencies the Lords | Justices in Council, confirming several | Acts and Laws of the Province of the | Massachusetts-Bay, made in the years, | 1694, 1695, 1696, 1697. | Published at Boston, April 27th. 1699.

Boston in New-England, Printed by Bartholomew Green and | John Allen, Printers to the Governour and Council. | 1699.

Collation: No title; pp. 1–4. W.

1699.

Acts | and | Laws, | Of His | Majesties Province of the Massachusetts- | Bay, in | New England. | [Royal Arms.]

Boston. | Printed by Bartholomew Green, and John Allen, (Printers | to His Excellency the Governour and Council,) | for, and Sold by Michael Perry at his Shop over against | the Town-House, and Benjamin Eliot under the West- | End of the Town-House. 1699.

Collation: Title to Charter, 1 leaf; Charter, pp. 3–15 [1]; Table, pp. (8); Title to Acts, 1 p.; Authorization, 1 p.; Acts, pp. 3–158; Table, pp. (4).

A. B. C. H. L. M. P. S. W.

The American Antiquarian Society's copy lacks Table, pp. (8). The Boston Athenæum copy lacks Table, pp. (8). The Harvard College Library copy has Title and pp. 3–6 torn. The Massachusetts Historical Society's copy lacks Charter and Tables. Title to Charter reads:

The | Charter | Granted by their Majesties | King William | and | Queen Mary, | To the | Inhabitants | Of the | Province | of the | Massachusetts-Bay | in | New-England. | Boston in New England. | Printed by Bartholomew Green, and John Allen, (Printers to His Excellency | the Governor & Council,) for, and Sold | by Michael Perry, and Benjamin Eliot. | 1699.[1]

1700.

Acts and Laws, | Passed by the Great and General Court or Assembly of the | Province of the Massachusetts-Bay in New-England: Begun and | Held at Boston, the Thirty-first of May, 1699. And continued | by several Prorogations unto Wednesday the Thirteenth of | March following, and then Sat.

Collation: No title; pp. 159–176.

A. B. C. H. L. M. P. S. W.

1700.

[Royal Arms.] | At | a Great and General Court or Assembly | of His Majesties Province of the Massachusetts-Bay in | New-England, begun and held at Boston upon Wednesday the | thirty-first day of May 1699. and continued by several | Prorogations unto Wednesday the Thirteenth day of March following. | In the Twelfth Year of His Majesties Reign.

Colophon: Boston, Printed by Bartholomew Green, and John Allen, Printers | to His Excellency the Governour and Council. 1700.

Collation: No title; pp. 6. P.

An Act for granting unto His Majesty a Tax upon Polls and Estates.

1700.

[Royal Arms.] | Acts and Laws, | Passed by the Great and General Court or Assembly of His Majesties | Province of the Massachusetts-Bay, in New England: Begun and |

[1] This volume, when complete, extends to p. 406.

Held at Boston, on Wednesday the Twenty-ninth of May, 1700.

Collation: No title; pp. 177–192.

A. B. C. H. L. M. P. S. W.

The Boston Athenæum copy lacks pp. 189, 190, and has pp. 177, 178, torn. Some copies have the Arms of William, others those of Anne, on p. 177. The Boston Public Library and the Lenox Library have both editions.

1701.

[Royal Arms.] | Acts and Laws, | Passed by the Great and General Court or Assembly of the | Province of the Massachusetts-Bay in New-England: Begun and | Held at Boston, the Twenty-ninth of May, 1700. And continued | by several Prorogations unto Wednesday the Twelfth of | February following and then Sat.

Collation: No title; pp. 193–204.

A. B. C. H. L. M. P. S. W.

The Boston Athenæum copy has pp. 193, 194, torn. Some copies have the Arms of William, others those of Anne, on p. 193. The Lenox Library has both editions.

1700.

[Royal Arms.] | At | a Great and General Court or Assembly | Of His Majesties Province of the Massachusetts-Bay in New-England, | Begun and Held at Boston upon Wednesday the Twenty-ninth | of May, 1700.

Colophon: Boston, Printed by B. Green, & J. Allen, Printers to His Excellency | the Governour and Council. 1700.

Collation: No title; pp. 4. P.

An Act for Granting unto His Majesty a Tax upon Polls and Estates.

1701.

Order of His Majesty in Council, Confirm- | ing several Acts & Laws of the Province | of the Massachusetts-Bay, made from the | 15th. of December 1697. to the 13th. of | March $\frac{1699}{1700}$. | Published at Boston, May 15th. 1701.

Boston in New England: | Printed by Bartholomew Green, and John Allen, Printers | to the Governour and Council. | 1701.

Collation: No title; pp. 4. B. C. H. L. S.

1701.

[Royal Arms.] | Acts and Laws, | Passed by the Great and General Court or Assembly of His Majesties | Province of the Massachusetts-Bay in New-England: Begun and Held | at Boston upon Wednesday the Twenty-eighth of May, 1701.

Collation: No title, pp. 205-223 [1].

A. B. C. H. L. M. P. S. W.

The Boston Athenæum copy lacks pp. 219–223, and has pp. 205, 206, torn. Some copies have the Arms of William, others those of Anne, on p. 205. The Boston Public Library and the Lenox Library have both editions.

1701.

[Royal Arms.] | At a Great and General Court or Assembly | of His Majesties Province of the Massachusetts-Bay in New-England: | Begun and Held at Boston upon Wednesday the Twenty-eighth of | May, 1701.

Colophon: Boston: | Printed by Bartholomew Green, and John Allen, Printers to the | Governour and Council. 1701.

Collation; No title; pp. 4. P.

An Act for Granting unto His Majesty a Tax upon Polls and Estates.

1701.

Order of His Majesty in Council, Confirm- | ing several Acts & Laws of the Province | of the Massachusetts-Bay in New-England, | past by the General Assembly, held the | 29th. of May. 1700. | Published at Boston, September 25. 1701.

Boston in New-England. | Printed by Bartholomew Green, and John Allen, Printers to His | Majesties Council of the Massachusetts Bay. | 1701.

Collation: No title; pp. 2. B. C. W.

1702.

[Royal Arms.] | Acts and Laws, | Passed by the Great and General Court or Assembly of Her | Majesties Province of the Massachusetts-Bay in New-England: | Begun and Held at Boston, upon Wednesday the | Twenty-seventh of May 1702.

Collation: No title; pp. 225–228.

A. B. C. H. L. M. P. S. W.

The Boston Athenæum copy has pp. 225, 226, torn.

1702.

[Royal Arms.] | At a Great and General Court or Assembly | of Her Majesties Province of the Massachusetts-Bay in New- | England: Begun and Held at Boston, upon Wednesday | the Twenty-seventh of May 1702.

Colophon: Boston: Printed by Bartholomew Green, and John Allen, Printers to | His Excellency the Governour and Council. 1702.

Collation: No title; pp. 4. P.

An Act for Granting unto His Majesty a Tax upon Polls and Estates.

1702.

[Royal Arms.] | Acts and Laws, | Passed by the Great and General Court or Assembly of Her | Majesties Province of the Massachusetts-Bay in New-England: Begun | and Held at Boston upon Wednesday the Twenty-seventh of May, | 1702. And continued by several Prorogations unto

Thursday, the | Fifteenth of October following, and then Sat at Cambridge.

Collation: No title; pp. 229–239 [1].

A. B. C. H. L. M. P. S. W.

The Boston Athenæum copy has pp. 229, 230, torn.

1702–03.

[Royal Arms.] | Acts and Laws, | Passed by the Great and General Court or Assembly of Her Majesties | Province of the Massachusetts-Bay, in New England: Begun and | Held at Boston, on Wednesday the Tenth of March, 1702.

Collation: No title; pp. 241–244. A. B. C. H. L. M. P. S. W.

The Boston Athenæum copy lacks pp. 241, 242.

1703.

[Royal Arms.] | Acts & Laws, | Passed by the Great and General Court or Assembly of Her | Majesties Province of the Massachusetts-Bay in New-England: | Begun and Held at Boston, upon Wednesday the Twenty-sixth | of May, 1703. And continued upon Adjournment unto | Wednesday the 30th. of June following, and then met.

Collation: No title; pp. 245, 246. A. B. C. H. L. M. P. S. W.

The Boston Athenæum copy is mutilated.

1703.

[Royal Arms.] | Acts, | Passed by the Great and General Court or Assembly of Her | Majesties Province of the Massachusetts-Bay in New-England: | Begun and Held at Boston upon Wednesday the Twenty-sixth | of May, 1703. And continued by Adjournment and Prorogation | unto Wednesday the First of September, following, and then met.

Collation: No title; pp. 247–253 [1].

A. B. C. H. L. M. P. S. W.

The Boston Athenæum copy has pp. 247, 248, mutilated.

1703.

[Royal Arms.] | Acts & Laws, | Passed by the Great and General Court or Assembly of Her | Majesties Province of the Massachusetts-Bay in New-England: | Begun and Held at Boston upon Wednesday the Twenty-sixth | of May 1703. And continued by Adjournment and Prorogations | unto Wednesday the Twenty-seventh of October following, | and then met.

Collation: No title; pp. 255–260. A. B. C. L. M. P. S. W.

The Boston Athenæum copy has pp. 255, 256, mutilated.

1703-04.

[Royal Arms.] | An Act, | Passed by the Great and General Court or Assembly of Her | Majesties Province of the Massachusetts-Bay in New England: | Begun and Held at Boston upon Wednesday the Twenty-sixth | of May 1703. And continued by adjournment and several Pro- | rogations unto Wednesday the Eighth of March following; and | then met: Being their fourth Session.

Collation: No title; pp. 261, 262. B. L. P. W.

The copies in the American Antiquarian Society and the Pennsylvania Historical Society are in facsimile. The Lenox Library has two copies, one original, the other in facsimile. This facsimile was issued by Dr. George H. Moore.

1704.

[Royal Arms.] | Acts and Laws, | Passed by the Great and General Court or Assembly of Her | Majesties Province of the Massachusetts-Bay in New England: | Begun and Held at Boston upon Wednesday the Thirty-first | of May, 1704.

Collation: No title; pp. 263–266. A. B. C. H. L. P. S. W.

The Boston Athenæum copy is mutilated.

1704.

[Royal Arms.] | An Act, | Passed by the Great and General Court or Assembly of Her | Majesties Province of the Massachusetts-Bay in New-England: | Begun and Held at Boston upon Wednesday the Thirty-first | of May, 1704.

Colophon: Boston: | Printed by Bartholomew Green, Printer to His Excellency | the Governour and Council. 1704.

Collation: No title; pp. (2). W.

The American Antiquarian Society's copy is mutilated. In it Dr. Haven has written: "No other copy of this leaf is known to be extant. S. F. H." The leaf has no signature and is bound between pp. 274, 275; but apparently it ought to come between pp. 262, 263, or pp. 266, 267.

1704.

[Royal Arms.] | An Act, | Passed by the Great and General Court or Assembly of Her | Majesties Province of the Massachusetts-Bay in New-England: | Begun and Held at Boston upon Wednesday the Thirty-first | of May, 1704.

Colophon: Boston: Printed by B. Green, Printer to His Excellency the | Governour and Council. 1704.

Collation: No title; pp. (4). L.

An Act for Punishing of Officers and Souldiers, retained in Her Majesties Service, and under Pay.

1704.

[Royal Arms.] | An Act, | Passed by the Great and General Court or Assembly of Her | Majesties Province of the Massachusetts-Bay in New-England: | Begun and Held at Boston upon Wednesday the Thirty-first | of May, 1704. And continued by Prorogation unto Wed- | nesday the Sixteenth of August following, and then met.

Collation: No title; pp. 267–269 [1].

A. B. C. H. L. P. S. W.

The Boston Athenæum has only a fragment of p. 269.

1704.

[Royal Arms.] | An Act, | Passed by the Great and General Court or Assembly of Her | Majesties Province of the Massachusetts-Bay in New-England: | Begun and Held at Boston upon Wednesday the Thirty-first | of May, 1704. And continued by several Prorogations unto | Wednesday the Twenty-fifth of October following, and then met, | being their Third Session.

Collation: No title; pp. 271, 272. B. C. H. L. P. S. W.

1704.

[Royal Arms.] | An Act, | Passed by the Great and General Court or Assembly of Her | Majesties Province of the Massachusetts-Bay in New-England: | Begun and Held at Boston upon Wednesday the Thirty-first | of May, 1704. And continued by several Prorogations unto | Wednesday the Twenty-seventh of December following, and | then met; being their Fourth Session.

Collation: No title; pp. 273, 274. B. C. H. L. P. S. W.

1705.

[Royal Arms.] | Acts and Laws, | Passed by the Great and General Court or Assembly of Her | Majesties Province of the Massachusetts-Bay in New-England: | Begun and Held at Boston upon Wednesday the Thirtieth | of May, 1705.

Collation: No title; pp. 275–277 [1]. A. B. C. H. L. P. W.

The Boston Athenæum copy has pp. 275, 276, mutilated.

1705.

[Royal Arms.] | Acts and Laws, | Passed by the Great and General Court or Assembly of Her | Majesties Province of Massachusetts-Bay in New-England: | Begun and Held at Boston upon Wednesday the Thirtieth | of May, 1705. And continued by several Prorogations | unto Wednesday the Twenty-fourth of October following, and | then met, being their Third Session.

Collation: No title; pp. 279–289 [1]. A. B. C. H. L. P. W.

The Boston Athenæum copy has pp. 279, 280, mutilated, and p. 289 torn.

1706.

[Royal Arms.] | Acts and Laws, | Passed by the Great and General Court or Assembly of Her | Majesties Province of the Massachusetts-Bay in New England: | Begun and Held at Boston upon Wednesday the Twenty ninth | Day of May, 1706.

Collation: No title; pp. 291–296. A. B. H. L. P.

The Boston Athenæum copy has pp. 291, 292, mutilated.[1]

1706.

[Royal Arms.] | An Act, | Passed by the Great and General Court or Assembly of Her | Majesties Province of the Massachusetts-Bay in New-England: Begun and Held at Boston upon Wednesday the Twenty-ninth | Day of May, 1706.

Colophon: Boston: Printed by B. Green, Printer to His Ex. the Gov. & Council. 1706.

Collation: No title; pp. (4). P.

An Act for Apportioning and Assessing of four several Taxes on Polls and Estates, Pursuant to the Funds and Grants made to Her Majesty, by the General Assembly in the years 1704, 1705, 1706.

---

[1] In 1866 fifty copies of pp. 291–366, edited by Ellis Ames, were printed in imitation of the original. Of this reprint, the American Antiquarian Society has pp. 291–363, the Boston Public Library has pp. 291–366, and the Harvard College Library has pp. 291–366, while various pages are found in other libraries. Unless otherwise specified, items noted in the text are originals.

1706.

[Royal Arms.] | An Act, | Passed by the Great and General Court or Assembly of Her | Majesties Province of the Massachusetts-Bay in New-England: | Begun and Held at Boston upon Wednesday the Twenty-ninth | of May, 1706. And continued by Prorogation unto Wed- | nesday the Seventh of August following, and then met.

Collation: No title; pp. 297, 298. B. H. L. P.

1706.

[Royal Arms.] | An Act, | Passed by the Great and General Court or Assembly of Her | Majesties Province of the Massachusetts-Bay in New-England: | Begun and Held at Boston upon Wednesday the Twenty-ninth | of May, 1706. And continued by Prorogation unto Wed- | nesday the Seventh of August following, and then met.

Collation: No title; pp. 299, 300. B. H. L. P.

1706.

[Royal Arms.] | Acts and Laws, | Passed by the Great and General Court or Assembly of Her | Majesties Province of the Massachusetts-Bay in New-England: | Begun and Held at Boston upon Wednesday the Twenty-ninth | of May, 1706. And continued by several Prorogations unto | Wednesday the Twenty-third of October following, and then met.

Collation: No title; pp. 301–304. A. B. H. L. P.

The Boston Athenæum copy lacks pp. 301, 302, and has pp. 303, 304, torn.

1707.

[Royal Arms.] | An Act, | Passed by the Great and General Court or Assembly of Her | Majesties Province of the

Massachusetts-Bay in New England: | Begun and Held at Boston upon Wednesday the Twenty-ninth | of May 1706. And continued by several Prorogations unto | Wednesday the Fifth of March following: and then met.

Collation: No title; p. 305 [1]. B. H. L. P.

1707.

[Royal Arms.] | Acts & Laws, | Passed by the Great and General Court or Assembly of Her | Majesties Province of the Massachusetts-Bay in New England: | Begun and Held at Boston upon Wednesday the Twenty-eighth | Day of May, 1707.

Collation: No title; pp. 307–310. B. H. L. P.

1707.

[Royal Arms.] | An Act, | Passed by the Great and General Court or Assembly of Her | Majesties Province of the Massachusetts-Bay in New-England: | Begun and Held at Boston upon Wednesday the Twenty-eighth | Day of May, 1707.

Colophon: Boston: Printed by B. Green, Printer to His Excel. the Governour & Council. 1707.

Collation: No title; pp. (4). P.

An Act for Apportioning and Assessing of Three several Taxes on Polls and Estates, Pursuant to the Funds and Grants made to Her Majesty by the General Assembly in the years 1705 and 1706.

1707.

[Royal Arms.] | Acts, | Passed by the Great and General Court or Assembly of Her | Majesties Province of the Massachusetts-Bay in New-England: | Begun and Held at Boston upon the Twenty-eighth | Day of May, 1707. And continued by Prorogation unto | Wednesday the Thirteenth of August following, and then met.

Collation: No title; pp. 311–313 [1]. B. H. L. P.

1707.

[Royal Arms.] | An Act, | Passed by the Great and General Court or Assembly of Her | Majesties Province of the Massachusetts-Bay in New-England: | Begun and Held at Boston upon Wednesday the Twenty-eighth | Day of May, 1707. And continued by several Prorogations | unto Wednesday the Twenty-ninth of October following, | and then met.

Collation: No title; pp. 315–318. B. H. L. P.

1707.

[Royal Arms.] | An Act, | Passed by the Great and General Court or Assembly of Her Majesties | Province of the Massachusetts-Bay in New-England, Begun and | Held at Boston upon Wednesday the Twenty-eighth Day of May, | 1707. And continued by several Prorogations unto Wednesday | the Twenty-ninth of October following, and then met.

Collation: No title; p. 319 [1]. B. H. L. P.

1708.

[Royal Arms.] | Acts and Laws, | Passed by the Great and General Court or Assembly of Her Majesties Province of the Massachusetts-Bay in New-England: | Begun and Held at Boston upon Wednesday the Twenty-sixth | Day of May, 1708.

Collation: No title; pp. 321–324. B. H. L. P. W.

The American Antiquarian Society's copy has pp. 321, 322, torn.

1708.

[Royal Arms.] | An Act, | Passed by the Great and General Court or Assembly of Her | Majesties Province of the

Massachusetts-Bay in New-England: | Begun and Held at Boston upon Wednesday the Twenty-sixth | Day of May, 1708.

Colophon: Boston: Printed by B. Green, Printer to His Ex. the Gov. & Council. 1708.

Collation: No title; pp. (4). P.

An Act for Apportioning and Assessing of Two several Taxes upon Polls and Estates, Pursuant to the Funds and Grants made to Her Majesty by the General Assembly in the Year, 1706.

1708.

[Royal Arms.] | Acts and Laws, | Passed by the Great and General Court or Assembly of Her | Majesties Province of the Massachusetts-Bay in New-England: | Begun and Held at Boston upon Wednesday the Twenty-sixth | Day of May, 1708. And continued by several Prorogations | unto Wednesday the Twentieth of October following, and then met.

Collation: No title; pp. 325–328. B. H. L. P.

The Harvard College Library has pp. 327, 328, torn.

1708.

[Royal Arms.] | Anno Sexto | Annæ | Reginæ.

Colophon: London, Printed by Charles Bill, and the Executrix of Thomas Newcomb, deceas'd, | Printers to the Queens Most Excellent Majesty. Reprinted at Boston in N. E. | by Bartholomew Green, Printer to His Excellency the Governour & Council. 1708.

Collation: No title; pp. 329–331 [1]. B. H. L. P. W.

An Act of Parliament for ascertaining the Rates of Foreign Coins in Her Majesties Plantations in America. The American Antiquarian Society's copy is torn.

1709.

[Royal Arms.] | Acts and Laws, | Passed by the Great and General Court or Assembly of Her | Majesties Province of the Massachusetts-Bay in New England: | Begun and Held at Boston upon Wednesday the Twenty-sixth | Day of May, 1708. And continued by several Prorogations | unto Wednesday the Sixteenth of February following, and then | met.

Collation: No title; pp. 333–335 [1]. A. B. H. L. P. W.

The Boston Athenæum copy has pp. 333, 334, mutilated.

1709.

[Royal Arms.] | Acts and Laws, | Passed by the Great and General Court or Assembly of Her | Majesties Province of the Massachusetts-Bay in New-England: | Begun and Held at Boston upon Wednesday the Twenty-fifth | Day of May, 1709.

Collation: No title; pp. 337–340. B. X. L. P. W.

1709.

[Royal Arms.] | An Act, | Passed by the Great and General Court or Assembly of Her | Majesties Province of the Massachusetts-Bay in New-England: | Begun and Held at Boston upon Wednesday the Twenty-fifth | Day of May, 1709.

Colophon: Boston: Printed by B. Green, Printer to His Excel. the Gov. & Council. 1709.

Collation: No title; pp. (4). P.

An Act for Apportioning and Assessing of Two several Taxes on Polls and Estates, Pursuant to the Funds and Grants made to Her Majesty, by the General Assembly, in the Year, 1707.

1709.

[Royal Arms.] | An Act, | Passed by the Great and General Court or Assembly of Her | Majesties Province of the Massachusetts-Bay in New-England: | Begun and Held at

Boston upon Wednesday the Twenty-fifth | Day of May 1709. And continued by several Prorogations | unto Wednesday the Twenty-sixth of October following, and | then met.

Collation: No title; pp. 341, 342. A. B. L. P. W.

The Boston Athenæum copy is mutilated. The Pennsylvania Historical Society's copy is a reprint.

1710.

[Royal Arms.] | Acts and Laws, | Passed by the Great and General Court or Assembly of Her | Majesties Province of the Massachusetts-Bay in New-England: | Begun and Held at Boston upon Wednesday the Twenty-fifth | Day of May 1709. And continued by several Prorogations | unto Wednesday the First of February following: and then met.

Collation: No title; pp. 343, 344. B. L. P. W.

The Pennsylvania Historical Society's copy is a reprint.

1710.

[Royal Arms.] | Acts and Laws, | Passed by the Great and General Court or Assembly of Her | Majesties Province of the Massachusetts-Bay in New-England: | Begun and Held at Boston upon Wednesday the Thirty-first | of May, 1710.

Collation: No title; pp. 345–354. B. L. P. W.

The Pennsylvania Historical Society's copy is a reprint.

1710.

[Royal Arms.] Acts and Laws, | Passed by the Great and General Court or Assembly of Her | Majesties Province of the Massachusetts-Bay in New-England: | Begun and Held at Boston upon Wednesday the Thirty-first | of May 1710. And continued by several Prorogations and | Adjournment unto Tuesday the Twenty-fourth of October | following, and then met.

Collation: No title; pp. 355–357 [1]. B. L. P. W.

The American Antiquarian Society's copy lacks p. 357. The Pennsylvania Historical Society's copy is a reprint.

1711.

[Royal Arms.] | Acts and Laws, | Passed by the Great and General Court or Assembly of Her | Majesties Province of the Massachusetts-Bay in New-England: | Begun and Held at Boston, upon Wednesday the Thirtieth Day | of May, 1711.

Collation: No title; pp. 359–362. B. L. P. W.

The American Antiquarian Society's copy is mutilated. The Pennsylvania Historical Society's copy is a reprint.

1711.

[Royal Arms.] | An Act, | Passed by the Great and General Court or Assembly of Her | Majesties Province of the Massachusetts-Bay in New-England: | Begun and Held at Boston upon Wednesday the Thirtieth Day | of May, 1711.

Colophon: Boston: Printed by B. Green, Printer to His Excellency the | Governour and Council. 1711.

Collation: No title; pp. (4). P.

An Act for Apportioning and Assessing of Three several Taxes on Polls and Estates, Pursuant to the Funds and Grants made to Her Majesty by the General Assembly, in the Years 1708 and 1709.

1711.

[Royal Arms.] | Acts and Laws, | Passed by the Great and General Court or Assembly of Her | Majesties Province of the Massachusetts-Bay in New-England: | Begun and Held at Boston upon Wednesday the Thirtieth Day of May, 1711. And continued by several Prorogations and | Adjournments unto Wednesday the Seventeenth of October | following, and then met.

Collation: No title; pp. 363–366. B. L.

1712.

[Royal Arms.] | Acts and Laws, | Passed by the Great and General Court or Assembly of Her | Majesties Province of the Massachusetts-Bay in New-England: | Begun and Held at Boston upon Wednesday the Thirtieth Day | of May, 1711. And continued by several Prorogations and | Adjournments unto Wednesday the Twelfth of March following, | and then met.

Collation: No title; pp. 367–376. B. L.

1712.

[Royal Arms.] | An Act, | Passed by the Great and General Court or Assembly of Her | Majesties Province of the Massachusetts-Bay in New-England: | Begun and Held at Boston upon Wednesday the Twenty-eighth | Day of May, 1712.

Collation: No title; pp. 377–379 [1]. L.

1712.

[Royal Arms.] | Acts and Laws, | Passed by the Great and General Court or Assembly of Her | Majesties Province of the Massachusetts-Bay in New-England: | Begun and Held at Boston upon Wednesday the Twenty-eighth | Day of May, 1712. And continued by several Prorogations unto | Wednesday the Twentieth of August following, and then met: | Being their Second Session.

Collation: No title; pp. 381–383 [1]. L.

1712.

[Royal Arms.] | Acts and Laws, | Passed by the Great and General Court or Assembly of Her | Majesties Province of the Massachusetts-Bay in New-England: | Begun and Held at Boston upon Wednesday the Twenty-eighth | of May, 1712. And continued by several Prorogations unto | Wednesday the Twenty-second of October following, and then | met Being their Third Session.

Collation: No title; pp. 385–387 [1]. L.

1713.

[Royal Arms.] | Acts and Laws, | Passed by the Great and General Court or Assembly of Her | Majesties Province of the Massachusetts-Bay in New-England: | Begun and Held at Boston upon Wednesday the Twenty-eighth | of May, 1712. And continued by several Prorogations unto | Wednesday the Eighteenth of March following, and then met: | Being their Fourth Session.

Collation: No title; pp. 389–391 [1]. L.

1713.

[Royal Arms.] | An Act, | Passed by the Great and General Court or Assembly of Her Majesties | Province of the Massachusetts-Bay in New-England: Begun and Held | at Boston upon Wednesday the Twenty-seventh Day of May, 1713.

Colophon: Boston: Printed by B. Green, Printer to His Excellency the | Governour and Council. 1713.

Collation: No title; pp. 4. P.

An Act for Apportioning and Assessing part of One Tax, and the whole of another Tax on Polls and Estates, Pursuant to the Funds and Grants made to Her Majesty by the General Assembly in the Year 1709, and part of another Tax made as aforesaid, in the Year 1710.

1713.

[Royal Arms.] | Acts and Laws, | Passed by the Great and General Court or Assembly of Her | Majesties Province of the Massachusetts-Bay in New-England: | Begun and Held at Boston upon Wednesday the Twenty-seventh | Day of May, 1713.

Collation: No title; pp. 393–396. L.

1713.

[Royal Arms.] | An Act, | Passed by the Great and General Court or Assembly of Her | Majesties Province of the Massachusetts-Bay in New-England: | Begun and Held at Boston upon Wednesday the Twenty-seventh | of May, 1713. And continued by Prorogations unto Wednes- | day the Fifth of August following, and then met: Being their Second Session.

Collation: No title; pp. 397, 398. L.

1713.

[Royal Arms.] | Acts and Laws, | Passed by the Great and General Court or Assembly of Her | Majesties Province of the Massachusetts-Bay in New-England: | Begun and Held at Boston upon Wednesday the Twenty-seventh | of May, 1713. And continued by several Prorogations unto | Wednesday the Fourteenth of October following, and then met: | Being their Third Session.

Collation: No title; pp. 399–406. L.

1713.

[Royal Arms.] | Province of the | Massachusetts=Bay. | An Act, | Made and Passed by the Great and General Court or | Assembly of Her Majesty's Province of the Massachusetts- | Bay in New=England, Held at Boston the 17th | Day of October, 1711.

Colophon: Boston, Printed by B. Green, Printer to His Excellency | the Governour and Council. 1713.

Collation: No title; pp. (2).

An Act to Reverse the Attainders of George Burroughs and others for Witchcraft. A facsimile of this Act, the original of which is in the possession of Mr. Abner C. Goodell, is given in 1 Proceedings of the Massachusetts Historical Society, xx. 284, 285; and in Dr. George H. Moore's Supplementary Notes on Witchcraft in Massachusetts, 1884, pp. 20, 21. Dr. Moore believed the alleged Act never became a law. See also 2 Proceedings of the Massachusetts Historical Society, i. 77–99, 99–118, 339–358.

1714.

Acts | and | Laws, | of Her Majesties | Province | of the | Massachusetts-Bay | in | New-England. | [Royal Arms.]

Boston in New-England: | Printed by B. Green, Printer to His Excellency the | Governour & Council, for Benjamin Eliot | and Sold at his Shop on the North side of King's Street. | 1714.

Collation: Title to Charter, 1 leaf; Charter, pp. 1–13 [1]; Table, pp. i–vi; Table (reprinted and covering the Session Laws to August, 1721, p. 360), pp. 1–16; Title to Acts, 1 p.; Authorization, 1 p.; Acts, pp. 1–239 [1]. B. C. H. J. L. M. P. S. W.

The American Antiquarian Society's copy lacks Table, pp. 1–16. The Boston Public Library has two copies, one lacking Table, pp. i–vi, the other lacking Table, pp. 1–16. The Harvard College Library copy lacks Title to Charter and Table, pp. 1–16, and has p. 13 of Charter torn. The Massachusetts Historical Society has two copies, one lacking Table, pp. 1–16, the other lacking Title to Charter, Table, pp. 1–16, Title, and Authorization. The John Carter Brown Library copy lacks Table, pp. 1–16. The Massachusetts State Library copy lacks Table, pp. i–vi. Title to Charter reads:

The | Charter | Granted by Their Majesties | King William | and | Queen Mary, | to the | Inhabitants | of the | Province | of the | Massachusetts-Bay | in | New-England | Boston in New-England: | Printed by B. Green, Printer to His Excellency the | Governor & Council, for Benjamin Eliot | and Sold at his Shop on the North side of King's Street. | 1714.[1]

1714.

[Royal Arms.] | Acts and Laws | Passed by the Great and General Court or Assembly of Her Majesties | Province of

[1] This volume, when complete, extends to p. 430.

the Massachusetts-Bay in New-England, Begun and Held | at Boston upon Wednesday the Twenty-sixth of May, 1714.

Collation: No title; pp. 241–247 [1].

B. C. L. M. P. S. W.

1714.

[Royal Arms.] | An Act, | Passed by the Great and General Court or Assembly of Her Majesties | Province of the Massachusetts-Bay in New-England, Begun and Held | at Boston upon Wednesday the Twenty-sixth of May, 1714.

Colophon: Boston: Printed by B. Green, Printer to His Excellency the Gov. & Council, 1714.

Collation: No title; pp. (4). P.

An Act for Apportioning and Assessing Two several Taxes on Polls and Estates, Pursuant to the Funds and Grants made to Her Majesty by the General Assembly, at their several Sessions in May and October, in the Year, 1710.

1714.

[Royal Arms.] | Acts and Laws | Passed by the Great and General Court or Assembly of His Majesties | Province of the Massachusetts-Bay in New-England; Begun and Held | at Boston upon Wednesday the Twenty-sixth of May, 1714. And | continued by several Prorogations unto Wednesday the Twentieth | of October following, and then met.

Collation: No title; pp. 249–252.

B. C. L. M. P. S. W.

1715.

[Royal Arms.] | Acts and Laws | Passed by the Great and General Court or Assembly of His Majesties | Province of the Massachusetts-Bay in New-England: Begun and Held | at Boston upon Wednesday the Twenty-fifth of May, 1715.

Collation: No title; pp. 253, 254. B. C. L. M. P. S. W.

1715.

[Royal Arms.] | Acts and Laws | Passed by the Great and General Court or Assembly of His Majesties | Province of the Massachusetts-Bay in New-England: Begun and Held | at Boston upon Wednesday the Twenty-fifth of May, 1715. And conti- | nued by Prorogation unto Wednesday the Twentieth Day of July | following, and then met.

Collation: No title; pp. 255–258. B. C. L. M. P. S. W.

1715.

[Royal Arms.] | Acts and Laws | Passed by the Great and General Court or Assembly of His Majesties | Province of the Massachusetts-Bay in New-England: Begun and Held | at Boston upon Wednesday the Twenty-fifth of May, 1715. And con- | tinued by several Prorogations unto Wednesday the Twenty-third | Day of November following, and then met.

Collation: No title; pp. 259–268.

B. C. L. M. P. S. W.

The Massachusetts Historical Society's copy has pp. 267, 268, torn.

1716.

[Royal Arms.] | Acts and Laws, | Passed by the Great and General Assembly of His Majesties | Province of the Massachusetts-Bay in New England: Begun and Held | at Boston upon Wednesday the Thirtieth of May, 1716.

Collation: No title; pp. 269–278. B. C. L. M. P. S. W.

1716.

[Royal Arms.] | Acts and Laws, | Passed by the Great and General Court of His Majesty's | Province of the Massachusetts-Bay in New England : Begun and | Held at Boston upon

Wednesday the Thirtieth of May, 1716. And | continued by several Prorogations unto Wednesday the Seventh | Day of November following, and then met.

Collation: No title; pp. 279–286. B. C. L. M. P. S. W.

1717.

[Royal Arms.] | Acts and Laws, | Passed by the Great and General Court or Assembly of His Majesty's | Province of the Massachusetts-Bay in New-England: Begun and | Held at Boston upon Wednesday the Twenty-ninth of May 1717.

Collation: No title; pp. 287–289 [1]. B. C. L. M. P. S. W.

1717.

[Royal Arms.] | Acts and Laws, | Passed by the Great and General Court or Assembly of His Majesty's | Province of the Massachusetts-Bay in New-England: Begun and | Held at Boston upon Wednesday the Twenty-ninth of May, 1717. | And continued by several Prorogations unto Wednesday the Twenty- | third of October following, and then Met.

Collation: No title; pp. 291–294. B. C. L. M. P. S. W.

1718.

[Royal Arms.] | Acts and Laws, | Passed by the Great and General Court or Assembly of His Majesty's | Province of the Massachusetts-Bay in New-England: Begun and | Held at Boston upon Wednesday the Twenty-ninth of May, 1717. | And continued by several Prorogations unto Thursday the Sixth | Day of February following, and then Met.

Collation: No title; pp. 295–298. B. C. L. M. P. S. W.

1718.

[Royal Arms.] | Acts and Laws, | Passed by the Great and General Court or Assembly of His Majesty's | Province of the Massachusetts-Bay in New-England: Begun and | Held at Boston upon Wednesday the Twenty-eighth of May, 1718.

Colophon: Boston: Printed by B. Green, Printer to His Excellency the | Governour & Council. 1718.

Collation: No title; pp. 299–309 [1]. B. C. L. P. S. W.

1718.

[Royal Arms.] | An Act | Passed by the Great and General Court or Assembly of His Majesty's Province | of the Massachusetts-Bay in New-England: Begun and Held at Boston upon | Wednesday the Twenty-eighth of May, 1718.

Colophon: Boston: Printed by B. Green, Printer to His Excellency the | Governour and Council. 1718.

Collation: No title; pp. (4). P.

An Act for Apportioning and Assessing a Tax of Eight Thousand Two Hundred and Fifty Pounds, upon Polls and Estates.

1718.

[Royal Arms.] | Acts and Laws | Passed by the Great and General Court or Assembly of His Majesty's | Province of the Massachusetts-Bay in New-England: Begun and | Held at Boston upon Wednesday the Twenty-eighth of May, 1718. | And continued by several Prorogations unto Wednesday the Twenty- | ninth Day of October following, and then Met.

Colophon: Boston: Printed by B. Green, Printer to His Excellency the | Governour and Council. 1718.

Collation: No title; pp. 311–314. B. C. L. P. S. W.

1719.

[Royal Arms.] | Acts and Laws | Passed by the Great and General Court or Assembly of His Majesty's | Province of the Massachusetts-Bay in New-England: Begun and Held |

at Boston upon Wednesday the Twenty-seventh Day of May, 1719.

Colophon: Boston: Printed by B. Green, Printer to His Excellency the | Governour and Council. 1719.

Collation: No title; pp. 315–318. B. C. L P. S. W.

1719.

[Royal Arms.] | An Act | Passed by the Great and General Court or Assembly of His Majesty's Province | of the Massachusetts-Bay in New-England: Begun and Held at Boston upon | Wednesday the Twenty-seventh Day of May, 1719.

Colophon: Boston: Printed by B. Green, Printer to His Excellency the | Gov. & Council. 1719.

Collation: No title; pp. (4). P.

An Act for Apportioning and Assessing a Tax of Four Thousand and Ten Pounds, Ten Shillings and Six Pence, upon Polls and Estates.

1719.

[Royal Arms.] | Acts and Laws | Passed by the Great and General Court or Assembly of His Majesty's | Province of the Massachusetts-Bay in New-England: Begun & Held | at Boston upon Wednesday the Twenty-seventh of May, 1719. | And continued by several Prorogations unto Wednesday the Fourth | Day of November following, and then Met.

Colophon: Boston: Printed by B. Green, Printer to His Excellency the | Governour and Council. 1719.

Collation: No title; pp. 319–326. B. C. L. P. S. W.

The Library of Congress copy lacks pp. 319, 320.

1720.

[Royal Arms.] | Acts and Laws | Passed by the Great and General Court or Assembly of His Majesty's | Province of

the Massachusetts-Bay in New England: Begun and | Held at Boston, upon Wednesday the Thirteenth Day of July, 1720.

Colophon: Boston: Printed by B. Green, Printer to His Excel. the Gover. & Council. 1720.

Collation: No title; pp. 327–330. B. L. P. S. W.

1720.

[Royal Arms.] | An Act | Passed by the Great and General Court or Assembly of His Majesty's Province | of the Massachusetts-Bay in New-England: Begun and Held at Boston, upon | Wednesday the Thirteenth Day of July, 1720.

Colophon: Boston: Printed by B. Green, Printer to His Excellency the Gov. & Council. 1720.

Collation: No title; pp. (4). P.

An Act for Apportioning and Assessing a Tax of Six Thousand Pounds, Seventeen Shillings and Three Pence, upon Polls and Estates.

1720.

[Royal Arms.] | Acts and Laws, | Passed by the Great and General Court or Assembly of His Majesty's | Province of the Massachusetts-Bay in New-England; Begun and | Held at Boston, upon Wednesday the Thirteenth Day of July, 1720. | And continued by several Prorogations unto Wednesday the Second | Day of November following, and then Met.

Colophon: Boston: Printed by B. Green, Printer to His Excellency the | Governour and Council. 1720.

Collation: No title; pp. 331–338. B. L. P. S. W.

1721.

[Royal Arms.] | Acts and Laws, | Passed by the Great and General Court or Assembly of His Majesty's | Province of the Massachusetts-Bay in New-England; Begun and | Held at Boston, upon Wednesday the Thirteenth Day of July, 1720. | And continued by several Prorogations unto Wednesday the | Fifteenth Day of March following, and then Met.

Colophon: Boston: Printed by B. Green, Printer to His Excellency the | Governour and Council. 1721.

Collation: No title; pp. 339–345 [1]. B. L. P. S. W.

1721.

[Royal Arms.] | An Act, | Passed by the Great and General Court or Assembly of His Majesty's | Province of the Massachusetts-Bay in New-England: Begun at | Boston, upon Wednesday the Thirty-first Day of May, 1721. | And continued by Adjournment to Cambridge, in the County of | Middlesex, unto Tuesday the Sixth Day of June following, | and then Met.

Colophon: Boston: Printed by B. Green, Printer to His Excellency the | Governour and Council. 1721.

Collation: No title; pp. 347–350. B. L. P. S.

1721.

[Royal Arms.] | Acts and Laws | Passed by the Great and General Court or Assembly of His Majesty's | Province of the Massachusetts-Bay in New-England; Begun & Held | at Boston upon Wednesday the Twenty-third Day of August, 1721.

Colophon: Boston: Printed by B. Green, Printer to His Excellency the | Governour and Council. 1721.

Collation: No title; pp. 351–356, 1 leaf. B. L. P. S.

On the leaf is printed a Resolve dated September 4, 1721.

1721.

[Royal Arms.] | An Act, | Passed by the Great and General Court or Assembly of His Majesty's | Province of the

Massachusetts-Bay in New-England; Begun & Held | at Boston upon Wednesday the Twenty-third Day of August, 1721.

Collation: No title; pp. 357, 358. B. L. P. S.

1721.

[Royal Arms.] | An Act, | Passed by the Great and General Court or Assembly of His Majesty's | Province of the Massachusetts-Bay in New-England; Begun & Held | at Boston, upon Wednesday the Twenty-third Day of August, 1721. | And continued by several Prorogations unto Cambridge in the | County of Middlesex, unto Friday the Third Day of November | following, and then Met.

Colophon: Boston: Printed by B. Green, Printer to His Excellency the | Governour and Council. 1721.

Collation: No title; pp. 359, 360. B. L. P. S.

1721.

For John Baskett's edition of Charter, see his Acts and Laws, 1724.

1722.

[Royal Arms.] | Acts and Laws | Passed by the Great and General Court or Assembly of His Majesty's | Province of the Massachusetts-Bay in New England; Begun and | Held at Boston upon Wednesday the Thirtieth Day of May, 1722.

Colophon: Boston: Printed by B. Green, Printer to His Excellency the | Governour and Council. 1722.

Collation: No title; pp. 361–367 [1]. B. L. P. S.

1722.

[Royal Arms.] | An Act | Passed by the Great and General Court or Assembly of His Majesty's Province | of the

Massachusetts-Bay in New-England: Begun and Held at Boston upon | Wednesday the Thirtieth Day of May, 1722.

Colophon: Boston: Printed by B. Green, Printer to His Excellency the Gov. & Council. 1722.

Collation: No title; pp. (4). P.

An Act Apportioning and Assessing a Tax of Six Thousand Two hundred and Thirty Two Pounds, Thirteen Shillings and Eleven Pence.

1722.

[Royal Arms.] | Acts and Laws | Passed by the Great and General Court or Assembly of His Majesty's | Province of the Massachusetts-Bay in New-England: Begun and | Held at Boston upon Wednesday the Thirtieth Day of May, 1722. | And continued by Prorogation unto Wednesday the Eighth Day of | August following, and then Met.

Colophon: Boston: Printed by B. Green, Printer to His Excellency the | Governour and Council. 1722.

Collation: No title; pp. 369–372. B. L. P. S.

1723.

[Royal Arms.] | Acts and Laws | Passed by the Great and General Court or Assembly of His Majesty's | Province of the Massachusetts-Bay in New England, Begun and | Held at Boston upon Wednesday the Thirtieth Day of May, 1722. | And continued by several Prorogations unto Thursday the Fifteenth | Day of November following, and then Met.

Colophon: Boston: Printed by B. Green, Printer to His Honour the | Lieutenant Governour and Council. 1723.

Collation: No title; pp. 373–380. B. P.

1723.

[Royal Arms.] | Acts and Laws | Passed by the Great and General Court or Assembly of His Majesty's | Province of

the Massachusetts-Bay in New-England, Begun & Held | at Boston upon Wednesday the Twenty-ninth Day of May, 1723.

Colophon: Boston: Printed by B. Green, Printer to His Honour the | Lieutenant Governour and Council. 1723.

Collation: No title; pp. 381–386. B. L. P.

The Lenox Library copy lacks pp. 385, 386.

1723.

[Royal Arms.] | An Act | Passed by the Great and General Court or Assembly of His Majesty's Province | of the Massachusetts-Bay in New-England, Begun and Held at Boston upon | Wednesday the Twenty-ninth Day of May, 1723.

Colophon: Boston: Printed by B. Green, Printer to His Honour the Lieut. Gov. & Council. 1723.

Collation: No title; pp. (4). P.

An Act for Apportioning and Assessing a Tax of Six Thousand Two Hundred and Five Pounds, Fifteen Shillings & Seven-pence Half Penny.

1723.

[Royal Arms.] | Acts and Laws | Passed by the Great and General Court or Assembly of His Majesty's | Province of the Massachusetts-Bay in New-England, Begun & Held | at Boston upon Wednesday the Twenty-ninth Day of May, 1723. | And continued by Prorogation unto Wednesday the Seventh Day of | August following, and then Met.

Colophon: Boston: Printed by B. Green, Printer to His Honour the | Lieutenant Governour and Council. 1723.

Collation: No title; pp. 387–392. B. P.

1723.

[Royal Arms.] | Acts and Laws | Passed by the Great and General Court or Assembly of His Majesty's | Province of

the Massachusetts-Bay in New England, Begun & Held | at Boston upon Wednesday the Twenty-ninth Day of May, 1723. | And continued by several Prorogations unto Wednesday the | Twenty-third Day of October following, and then Met.

Colophon: Boston: Printed by B. Green, Printer to His Honour the | Lieutenant Governour and Council. 1723.

Collation: No title; pp. 393–395 [1]. B. P.

1724.

[Royal Arms.] | An Act | Passed by the Great and General Court or Assembly of His Majesty's | Province of the Massachusetts-Bay in New-England, Begun and Held | at Boston upon Wednesday the Twenty-seventh Day of May, 1724.

Colophon: Boston: Printed by B. Green, Printer to His Honour the Lieut. Governour | and Council. 1724.

Collation: No title; p. 397 [1]. B. P.

1724.

[Royal Arms.] | An Act | Passed by the Great and General Court or Assembly of His Majesty's Province | of the Massachusetts-Bay in New-England, Begun and Held at Boston upon | Wednesday the Twenty-seventh Day of May, 1724.

Colophon: Boston: Printed by B. Green, Printer to His Honour the Lieut. Gov. & Council. 1724.

Collation: No title; pp. (4). P.

An Act for Apportioning and Assessing a Tax of Fourteen Thousand Pounds.

1724.

Acts and Laws, | Passed by the | Great and General Court or Assembly | Of the Province of the | Massachusetts-Bay | in | New-England, | From 1692, to 1719. | To which is Prefix'd, | The Charter, Granted by Their late | Majesties King William and Queen Mary, to the | Inhabitants of the said Province, A.D. 1691, | Annoq; Regni 3°. | [Royal Arms.]

London, | Printed by John Baskett, Printer to the King's most Excellent | Majesty, MDCCXXIV.

Collation: Title, 1 leaf; Index, pp. iii–xvi; Title to Charter, 1 leaf; Charter, pp. iii–xvi; Acts, pp. 1–359 [1]. A. B. H[L]. J. L. M. N. P. S. W.

Title to Charter reads:

The | Charter | Granted by Their Majesties | King William and Queen Mary, | to the | Inhabitants | of the | Province of the Massachusetts-Bay | in | New-England. | [Royal Arms.] | London, | Printed by John Baskett, Printer to the King's most Ex- | cellent Majesty, And by the Assigns of Thomas Newcomb, | and Henry Hills, deceas'd. MDCCXXI.

1725.

[Royal Arms.] | Acts and Laws | Passed by the Great and General Court or Assembly of His Majesty's | Province of the Massachusetts-Bay in New-England, Begun & Held | at Boston upon Wednesday the Twenty-seventh of May, 1724. | And continued by several Prorogations unto Wednesday the | Eleventh Day of November following, and then Met.

Colophon: Boston: Printed by B. Green, Printer to His Honour the | Lieutenant Governour and Council, 1725

Collation: No title; pp. 399–411 [1]. B. P.

The Boston Public Library copy lacks p. 411.

1725.

At a Great and | General Court | or | Assembly | For His Majesty's Province of the Massa- | chusetts-Bay in New-England, begun & held | at Boston, upon Wednesday, May 25th. 1725.

Collation: No title; 1 leaf, unpaged. B.

Relating to the salaries of ministers. A facsimile of this Resolve, of which the original is in the Chamberlain Collection in the Boston Public Library, is given in the Publications of this Society, viii. 130, 131.

1725.

[Royal Arms.] | Acts and Laws | Passed by the Great and General Court or Assembly of His Majesty's | Province of the Massachusetts-Bay in New-England, Begun & Held | at Boston upon Wednesday the Twenty-sixth Day of May 1725. | And continued by several Prorogations unto Wednesday the | Third Day of November following, and then Met.

Colophon: Boston: Printed by B. Green, Printer to His Honour the | Lieutenant Governour and Council. 1725.

Collation: No title; pp. 413–422. B. L. P. S.

1726.

[Royal Arms.] | Acts and Laws | Passed by the Great and General Court or Assembly of His Majesty's | Province of the Massachusetts-Bay in New-England, Begun and Held | at Boston, upon Wednesday the Twenty-fifth Day of May, 1726.

Colophon: Boston: Printed by B. Green, Printer to His Honour the | Lieutenant Governour & Council. 1726.

Collation: No title; pp. 423–430. P. S.

1726.

Acts | and | Laws, | Of His Majesty's | Province | of the | Massachusetts-Bay | in | New-England. | [Royal Arms.]

Boston in New-England: | Printed by B. Green, Printer to the Honourable the Lieut. | Governour & Council, for Benjamin Eliot, | and Sold at his Shop near the Town-House in King's-Street. | 1726.

Collation: Title to Charter, 1 leaf; Charter, pp. 1–12; Explanatory Charter, pp. 13, 14; Table, pp. 1–17 [1]; Title to Acts, 1 p.; Authorization, 1 p.; Acts, pp. 1–347 [1]. A. B. C. H. J. L. M. N. P. S. W.

The John Carter Brown copy was a presentation copy from Governor Belcher to the Earl of Ilay, 1732. The Massachusetts Historical Society's copy lacks

Title to Charter, Charter, Explanatory Charter, and Table, pp. 1–10, and has pp. 345, 346, torn. Title to Charter reads:

The | Charter | Granted by Their Majesties | King William | and | Queen Mary, | to the | Inhabitants | of the | Province | of the | Massachusetts-Bay | in | New-England. | Boston in New-England: | Printed by B. Green, Printer to the Honourable the Lieut. | Governour & Council, for Benjamin Eliot, | and Sold at his Shop near the Town-House in King's Street. | 1726.[1]

1727.

[Royal Arms.] | Acts and Laws, | Passed by the Great and General Court or Assembly of His Majesty's | Province of the Massachusetts Bay in New-England; Begun and | Held at Boston upon Wednesday the Twenty-fifth Day of May, 1726. | And continued by several Prorogations unto Wednesday the Twenty- | third Day of November following, and then Met.

Colophon: Boston: Printed by B. Green, Printer to the Honourable the Lieut. | Governour & Council, for Benjamin Eliot. 1727.

Collation: No title; pp. 349–354.

A. B. C. H. J. L. M. N. P. S. W.

1727.

[Royal Arms.] | Acts and Laws, | Passed by the Great and General Court or Assembly of His Majesty's | Province of the Massachusetts-Bay in New-England, Begun and Held | at Boston, upon Wednesday the Thirty-first Day of May, 1727.

Colophon: Boston: Printed by B. Green, Printer to His Honour the Lieut. | Governour & Council, for Benjamin Eliot. 1727.

Collation: No title; pp. 355–370.

A. B. C. H. J. L. N. P. S. W.

1727.

[Royal Arms.] | Acts and Laws, | Passed by the Great and General Court or Assembly of His Majesty's | Province of

[1] This volume, when complete, extends to p. 789.

the Massachusetts-Bay in New-England, Begun and Held | at Boston, upon Wednesday the Thirty-first Day of May, 1727. | And continued by Adjournment to the Sixteenth Day of August | following.

Colophon: Boston: Printed by B. Green, Printer to His Honour the Lieut. | Governour & Council, for Benjamin Eliot. 1727.

Collation: No title; pp. 371–373 [1].

A. B. C. H. J. L. M. N. P. S. W.

1727.

An Act | passed by the Great and General Court or Assembly of His Majesty's Province | of the Massachusetts-Bay in New-England, Begun and Held at Boston upon | Wednesday the Thirty-first Day of May, 1727. And continued by several | Adjournments unto Wednesday the Fourth Day of October following.

Colophon: Boston: Printed by B. Green, Printer to His Honour the Lieut. Gov. & Council. 1727.

Collation: No title; pp. (7). S.

An Act for Apportioning and Assessing a Tax of Six Thousand Pounds, etc.

1728.

[Royal Arms.] | An Act | Passed by the Great and General Court or Assembly of His Majesty's | Province of the Massachusetts-Bay in New-England, Begun and | Held at Boston, upon Wednesday the Thirty-first Day of May, | 1727. And continued by several Adjournments unto Wednesday | the Fourth Day of October following.

Collation: No title; pp. 375, 376.

A. B. C. H. J. L. M. N. P. S. W.

1728.

[Royal Arms.] | Acts and Laws | Passed by the Great and General Court or Assembly of His Majesty's | Province of

the Massachusetts-Bay in New-England, Begun and | Held at Boston, upon Wednesday the Twenty-second Day of | November, 1727.

Colophon: Boston: Printed by B. Green, Printer to His Honour the Lieut. Gov. & Council. | 1728.

Collation: No title; pp. 377–400.

A. B. C. H. J. L. M. N. P. S. W.

1728.

[Royal Arms.] | Acts and Laws | Passed by the Great and General Court or Assembly of His Majesties | Province of the Massachusetts-Bay in New-England, Begun and Held | at Boston upon Wednesday the Twenty-ninth Day of May, 1728.

Colophon: Boston: Printed by B. Green, Printer to His Honour the Lieut. | Governour & Council, for Benjamin Eliot. 1728.

Collation: No title; pp. 401–412.

A. B. C. H. J. L. M. N. P. S. W.

1728.

Anno Regni Regis Georgii II. Primo & Secundo.

Colophon: Boston: Printed by B. Green, Printer to His Honour the Lieutenant | Governour and Council. 1728.

Collation: No title; pp. (5). S.

This is a Tax List, but as the Massachusetts State Library copy lacks pp. 1, 2, the caption cannot be given.

1728.

[Royal Arms.] | Acts and Laws | Passed by the Great and General Court or Assembly of His Majesties | Province of the Massachusetts-Bay in New-England, Begun and Held | at Boston upon Wednesday the Twenty-ninth Day of May, 1728. | And continued by Prorogation unto Wednesday the Twenty-fourth | Day of July following, and then Met.

Collation: No title; pp. 413–416.

A. B. C. H. J. L. M. N. P. S. W.

An act passed at this Session was omitted in the printing, but is given on page 425 issued in a later Session. See p. 68, below.

1729.

[Royal Arms.] | An Act | Passed by the Great and General Court or Assembly of His Majesties | Province of the Massachusetts-Bay in New-England, Begun & Held | at Boston upon Wednesday the Twenty-ninth Day of May, 1728. | And continued by several Prorogations and Adjournments to Salem | the Second of April, 1729.

Collation: No title; pp. 417–419 [1].

A. B. H. J. L. M. N. P. S. W.

These pages also contain the Acts and Laws passed at the August Session held at Cambridge, August 27, 1729.

1729.

[Royal Arms.] | An Act | Passed by the Great and General Court or Assembly of His Majesties Province | of the Massachusetts-Bay in New-England, Begun and Held at Salem upon | Wednesday the Twenty-eighth Day of May 1729. And continued by several | Prorogations and Adjournment to Cambridge the Twenty-seventh Day of | August following.

Colophon: Boston: Printed by B. Green, Printer to His Honour the Lieutenant | Governour and Council. 1729.

Collation: No title; pp. 5 [7]. P. S.

An Act for Apportioning and Assessing a Tax of Eight Thousand Two Hundred and Eight Pounds, and also . . . a further Tax of Four Thousand Six Hundred and Forty Three Pounds Sixteen Shillings, paid the Representatives, Anno 1728.

1729.

A | Collection | Of the Proceedings of the | Great and General Court or Assembly | Of His Majesty's Province of the | Massachusetts-Bay | in New-England; | Containing several Instructions from the Crown, to the | Council and Assembly of that Province, for fixing a | Salary on the Governour, and their Determinations | thereon. | As also, | The Methods taken by the Court for Supporting the several | Governours, since the Arrival of the present Charter. | Printed by Order of the House of Representatives. | [Cut.]

Boston: Printed by T. Fleet, in Pudding-Lane. | 1729.

Collation: Title, 1 leaf; Text, pp. 3–112. A. H. M. W.

1730.

[Royal Arms.] | Acts and Laws | Passed by the Great and General Court or Assembly of His Majesties | Province of the Massachusetts-Bay in New-England, Begun and | Held at Salem upon Wednesday the Twenty-eighth Day of May, | 1729. And continued by several Prorogations and Adjournments | to Boston the Nineteenth Day of November following.

Collation: No title; pp. 421–425.

A. B. C. H. J. L. M. N. P. S. W.

Printed with the next item.

1730.

[Royal Arms.] | Acts and Laws | Passed by the Great and General Court or Assembly of His Majesty's | Province of the Massachusetts-Bay in New-England: Begun and | Held at Cambridge upon Wednesday the Twenty-seventh Day of | May, 1730. and continued by several Prorogations to Wednesday | the Ninth Day of September following, and continued by Adjourn- | ment to Roxbury and thence to Boston.

Collation: No title; pp. 426–436.

A. B. C. H. J. L. M. N. P. S. W.

Printed with the previous item.

1730.

[Royal Arms.] | An Act | Passed by the Great and General Court or Assembly of His Majesties Province | of the

Massachusetts-Bay in New-England, Begun and Held at Cambridge | upon Wednesday the Twenty-seventh Day of May 1730. And continued | by several Prorogations and Adjournment to the Ninth Day of September | following.

Colophon: Boston: Printed by B. Green, Printer to His Excellency the | Governour and Council. 1730.

Collation: No title; pp. 5 [7]. P.

An Act for Apportioning and Assessing a Tax of Eight Thousand Pounds, and also . . . a further Tax of Two Hundred Forty Pounds Thirteen Shillings laid on several Towns within mentioned for not sending a Representative as by Law they are obliged, and also . . . a further Tax of Two Thousand Three Hundred and Fifty-one Pounds Fifteen Shillings, paid the Representatives, Anno 1729.

1730–31.

[Royal Arms.] | Acts and Laws | Passed by the Great and General Court or Assembly of His Majesty's | Province of the Massachusetts-Bay in New-England: Begun and | Held at Boston upon Wednesday the Tenth Day of February, 1730.

Collation: No title; pp. 437–456.

A. B. C. H. J. L. M. N. P. S. W.

1731.

[Royal Arms.] | Acts and Laws | Passed by the Great and General Court or Assembly of His Majesties | Province of the Massachusetts-Bay in New-England, Begun & Held | at Boston, upon Wednesday the Twenty-sixth Day of May, 1731.

Collation: No title; pp. 457–462.

A. B. C. H. J. L. M. N. P. S. W.

1731.

[Royal Arms.] | An Act | Passed by the Great and General Court or Assembly of His Majesties Province | of the Massachusetts-Bay in New-England, Begun and Held at

Boston, upon | Wednesday the Twenty-sixth Day of May, 1731.

Colophon: Boston: Printed by B. Green, Printer to His Excellency the | Governour and Council. 1731.

Collation: No title; pp. 5 [7]. P.

An Act for Apportioning and Assessing a Tax of Six Thousand Eight Hundred and Eighteen Pounds.

1731.

[Royal Arms.] | Acts and Laws | Passed by the Great and General Court or Assembly of His Majesties | Province of the Massachusetts-Bay in New-England, begun & Held | at Boston, upon Wednesday the Twenty-sixth Day of May, 1731. | and continued by several Adjournments unto Wednesday the Third | Day of November following.

Collation: No title; pp. 463–468.

A. B. C.[1] H. J. L. M. N. P. S. W.

1732.

[Royal Arms.] | Acts and Laws | Passed by the Great and General Court or Assembly of His Majesty's | Province of the Massachusetts-Bay in New-England, Begun and | Held at Boston upon Wednesday the Twenty-sixth Day of May | 1731. and continued by several Adjournments and Prorogation | unto Wednesday the First Day of December following.

Collation: No title; pp. 469–476.

A. B. C. H. J. L. M. N. P. S. W.

1732.

[Royal Arms.] | Acts and Laws | Passed by the Great and General Court or Assembly of His Majesty's | Province of the Massachusetts-Bay in New-England, Begun & Held | at Boston upon Wednesday the Thirty-first Day of May, 1732.

Collation: No title; pp. 477–483 [1].

A. B. C. H. J. L. M. N. P. S. W.

1732.

[Royal Arms.] | An Act | Passed by the Great and General Court or Assembly of His Majesty's Province | of the Massachusetts-Bay in New-England, Begun and Held at Boston, upon | Wednesday the Thirty-first Day of May, 1732.

Colophon: Boston: Printed by B. Green, Printer to His Excellency the | Governour and Council. 1732.

Collation: No title; pp. 5 [7]. P. S.

An Act for Apportioning and Assessing a Tax of Eight Thousand and seven Pounds sixteen Shillings.

1733.

[Royal Arms.] | Acts and Laws | Passed by the Great and General Court or Assembly of His Majesty's | Province of the Massachusetts-Bay in New-England, begun and | Held at Boston upon Wednesday the Thirty-first Day of May 1732. | and continued by Adjournment unto Thursday the first Day of | November following.

Collation: No title; pp. 485–490.
A. B. C. H. L. M. N. P. S. W.

1733.

[Royal Arms.] | Acts and Laws | Passed by the Great and General Court or Assembly of His Majesty's | Province of the Massachusetts-Bay in New-England, begun & held | at Boston, upon Wednesday the Thirty-first Day of May, 1733 [for 1732]. | and continued by several Adjournments unto Wednesday the Fourth | Day of April following.

Collation: No title; pp. 491–498.
A. B. C. H. L. M. N. P. S. W.

1733.

[Royal Arms.] | An Act | Passed by the Great and General Court or Assembly of His Majesty's | Province of the Massachusetts-Bay in New-England; begun & held | at Boston, upon Wednesday the Thirtieth Day of May 1733.

Collation: No title; pp. 499, 500.

A. B. C. H. L. M. N. P. S. W.

1733.

[Royal Arms.] | An Act | Passed by the Great and General Court or Assembly of His Majesty's Province | of the Massachusetts-Bay in New-England, begun and held at Boston, upon | Wednesday the Thirtieth Day of May 1733.

Colophon: Boston: | Printed by John Draper, Printer to His Excellency the | Governour and Council. 1733.

Collation: No title; pp. (7). P. S.

An Act apportioning and assessing a Tax of Seven Thousand nine Hundred and Eighty seven Pounds sixteen Shillings.

1733.

[Royal Arms.] | Acts and Laws | Passed by the Great and General Court or Assembly of His Majesty's | Province of the Massachusetts-Bay in New England, begun & held | at Boston, upon Wednesday the Thirtieth Day of May 1733. | and continued by several Adjournments unto Wednesday the | Third Day of October following.

Collation: No title; pp. 501–508.

A. B. C. H. L. M. N. P. S. W.

1734.

Acts and Laws | Passed by the Great and General Court or Assembly of His Majesty's | Province of the Massachusetts-Bay in New-England, begun and held | at Boston, upon Wednesday the Thirtieth Day of May 1733, and | continued by several Adjournments unto Thursday the Twenty- | fourth Day of January following.

Collation: No title; pp. 509, 510.

A. B. C. H. L. M. N. P. S. W.

1734.

[Royal Arms.] | Acts and Laws | Passed by the Great and General Court or Assembly of His Majesty's | Province of the Massachusetts-Bay in New-England, begun and held | [at] Boston, upon Wednesday the Thirtieth Day of May 1733, and | continued by several Adjournments, unto Wednesday the Tenth | Day of April following.

Collation: No title; pp. 511, 512.

A. B. C. H. L. M. N. P. S. W.

1734.

[Royal Arms.] | Acts and Laws | Passed by the Great and General Court or Assembly of His Majesty's | Province of the Massachusetts-Bay in New-England, Begun and Held | at Boston, upon Wednesday the Twenty-ninth Day of May 1734.

Collation: No title; pp. 513–525 [1].

A. B. C. H. L. M. N. P. S. W.

1734.

[Royal Arms.] | An Act | Passed by the Great and General Court or Assembly of His Majesty's Province of the | Massachusetts Bay in New England, Begun and Held at Boston, upon Wednesday the | Twenty-ninth Day of May, 1734.

Colophon: Boston, | Printed by John Draper, Printer to His Excellency the | Governour and Council. 1734.

Collation: No title; pp. (9). S.

An Act for apportioning and assessing a Tax of Sixteen Thousand and fifteen Pounds and twelve Shillings.

1735.

[Royal Arms.] | Acts and Laws | Passed by the Great and General Court or Assembly of His Majesty's | Province of the Massachusetts Bay in New-England, begun and held | at

Boston, upon Wednesday the Twenty-ninth Day of May 1734, | and continued by Adjournments, unto Wednesday the Twentieth | Day of November following.

Collation: No title; pp. 527–530.

A. B. C. H. L. M. P. S. W.

1735.

[Royal Arms.] | Acts and Laws | Passed by the Great and General Court or Assembly of His Majesty's Pro- | vince of the Massachusetts-Bay in New-England, Begun and Held at Boston, | upon Wednesday the Twenty-ninth Day of May 1734, and continued | by Adjournments, unto Wednesday the Twentieth Day of November | following.

Collation: No title; pp. 527–530. L. N.

The text is identical with the preceding item, but the marginal notes are a little differently placed.

1735.

[Royal Arms.] | Acts and Laws | Passed by the Great and General Court or Assembly of His Majesty's Province | of the Massachusetts-Bay in New-England, begun and held at Boston, upon | Wednesday the Twenty-ninth Day of May 1734, and continued by | several Adjournments unto Wednesday the Ninth Day of April following.

Colophon: Boston: Printed by John Draper, Printer to His | Excellency the Governour and Council. [1735.]

Collation: No title; pp. 531–534.

A. B. C. H. L. M. N. P. S. W.

1735

[Royal Arms.] | Acts and Laws | Passed by the Great and General Court or Assembly of His Majesty's | Province of the Massachusetts-Bay in New-England, Begun and Held at |

Boston, upon Wednesday the Twenty-eighth Day of May 1735.

Colophon: Boston: Printed by J. Draper, Printer to His Excellency the Governour and Council. 1735.

Collation: No title; pp. 535–549 [1].

A. B. C. H. L. M. N. P. S. W.

1735.

[Royal Arms.] | An Act, | Passed by the Great and General Court or Assembly of His Majesty's Province of the Massachusetts-Bay in New-England, Begun and Held at Boston, upon Wednesday the | Twenty-eighth Day of May 1735.

Colophon: Boston: | Printed by John Draper, Printer to His Excellency the | Governour and Council. 1735.

Collation: No title; pp. (9). S.

An Act for apportioning and assessing a Tax of Thirty Thousand ninety-nine Pounds, fourteen Shillings and three Pence. The Massachusetts State Library copy is slightly torn.

1736.

[Royal Arms.] | Acts and Laws | Passed by the Great and General Court or Assembly of His Majesty's | Province of the Massachusetts-Bay in New-England, Begun and Held at | Boston, upon Wednesday the Twenty eighth Day of May 1735. | And continued by Adjournments to Wednesday the Nineteenth Day | of November following.

Colophon: Boston: Printed by J. Draper, Printer to His | Excellency the Governour and Council. [1736.]

Collation: No title; pp. 551–558.

A. B. C. H. L. M. N. P. S. W.

1736.

[Royal Arms.] | Acts and Laws | Passed by the Great and General Court or Assembly of His Majesty's Province | of the Massachusetts-Bay in New-England, begun and held at Boston, upon | Wednesday the Twenty-eighth Day of May 1735, and continued by | several Adjournments unto Wednesday the Seventeenth of March following.

Colophon: Boston: Printed by J. Draper, Printer to His | Excellency the Governour and Council. [1736.]

Collation: No title; pp. 559, 560.

A. B. C. H. L. M. N. P. S. W.

1736.

[Royal Arms.] | Acts and Laws | Passed by the Great and General Court or Assembly of His Majesty's | Province of the Massachusetts-Bay in New-England, begun and held at | Boston, upon Wednesday the Twenty-sixth Day of May 1736.

Colophon: Boston: | Printed by J. Draper, Printer to His Excellency the | Governour & Council. 1736.

Collation: No title; pp. 561–564.

A. B. C. H. L. M. N. P. S. W.

1736.

[Royal Arms.] | An Act | Passed by the Great and General Court or Assembly of His Majesty's Province of the Massachusetts- | Bay in New England, Begun and Held at Boston, upon Wednesday the Twenty-sixth Day of | May 1736.

Colophon: Boston: | Printed by John Draper, Printer to His Excellency the | Governour and Council. 1736.

Collation: No title; pp. (9). P. S.

An Act for apportioning and assessing a Tax of Twenty-nine Thousand nine Hundred and Fifty-three Pounds seven shillings and six Pence. "There are two pages each numbered 2, 3, and 4 respectively. The other pages are not numbered" (Hildeburn).

1736.

[Royal Arms.] | An Act | Passed by the Great and General Court or Assembly of His Majesty's | Province of the Massachusetts-Bay in New-England, begun and held at | Boston, upon Wednesday the Twenty-sixth Day of May 1736.

Colophon: Boston: Printed by John Draper, Printer to His Excellency | the Governour and Council. 1736.

Collation: No title; pp. (6). P.

An Act for granting unto His Majesty several Rates and Duties of Impost and Tunnage of Shipping.

1736.

Province of the | Massachusetts- | Bay, ss. | [Royal Arms.] | William Foye, Esq; | Treasurer and Receiver General of His Majesty's said Province, | To —— Constable or Collector of the Town of —— Greeting, &c.

Collation: No title; 1 leaf. P.

Notice issued under provision of the preceding item.

1737.

[Royal Arms.] | Acts and Laws | Passed by the Great and General Court or Assembly of His Majesty's | Province of the Massachusetts-Bay in New-England, begun and held at | Boston, upon Wednesday the Twenty-sixth Day of May 1736. And | continued by several Prorogations unto Wednesday the Twenty-fourth | Day of November following and then Met.

Colophon: Boston: Printed by John Draper, Printer to His | Excellency the Governour and Council. 1737.

Collation: No title; pp. 565–592.

A. B. C. H. L. M. N. P. S. W.

1737.

[Royal Arms.] | Acts and Laws | Passed by the Great and General Court or Assembly of His Majesty's Pro- | vince of the Massachusetts-Bay in New-England, Begun and Held at Boston, | upon Wednesday the Twenty-fifth Day of May 1737.

Colophon: Boston: Printed by J. Draper, Printer to His Excellency the | Governour and Council. [1737.]

Collation: No title; pp. 593–626.

A. B. C. H. L. M. N. P. S. W.

Page 617 is misnumbered 517. The Boston Athenæum and the New York Historical Society's copies lack pp. 625, 626. Some copies do not have the Figures of the Bills on p. 625.

1737.

[Royal Arms.] | An Act | Passed by the Great and General Court or Assembly of His Majesty's Province of the Massachusetts- | Bay in New-England, Begun and Held at Boston, upon Wednesday the Twenty-fifth Day of | May, 1737.

Colophon: Boston: | Printed by J. Draper, Printer to His Excellency the | Governour and Council.

Collation: No title; pp. (9). S.

An Act for apportioning and assessing a Tax of Forty four Thousand nine hundred and thirty Pounds one shilling and three pence.

1737.

[Royal Arms.] | Extract from | An Act | Passed by the Great and General Court or Assembly of His Majesty's Province of the | Massachusetts-Bay in New-England, Begun and Held at Boston, upon Wednesday the | Twenty-fifth Day of May, 1737. | Intitled, | An Act for supplying the Treasury with the Sum of Twenty | Thousand Pounds in

Bills of Credit of the New Tenor for dis- | charging the Publick Debts, &c. And for establishing the | wages of sundry Persons, &c. in the Service of the Province, | . . .

[Boston: John Draper. 1737.]

Collation: No title; pp. (7). P.

1738.

[Royal Arms.] | Acts and Laws | Passed by the Great and General Court or Assembly of His Majesty's Pro- | vince of the Massachusetts-Bay in New England, Begun and Held at Boston, | upon Wednesday the Twenty-fifth Day of May 1737. and continued by | Prorogation and Adjournments to Wednesday the 30th Day of November | following.

Colophon: Boston: | Printed by J. Draper, Printer to His Excellency the | Governour and Council. [1738.]

Collation: No title; pp. 627–644.

A. B. C. H. L. M. N. P. S. W.

1738.

[Royal Arms.] | Acts and Laws | Passed by the Great and General Court or Assembly of His Majesty's Pro- | vince of the Massachusetts-Bay in New England, Begun and Held at Boston, | upon Wednesday the Thirty-first Day of May, 1738.

Colophon: Boston: | Printed by John Draper, Printer to His Excellency the | Governour and Council. [1738.]

Collation: No title; pp. 645–664.

A. B. C. H. L. M. N. P. S. W.

The Massachusetts Historical Society's copy lacks pp. 653–664.

1738.

An Act | Pass'd by the Great and General Court or Assembly of His Majesty's Province | of the Massachusetts-

Bay in New-England, begun and held at Boston, | on Wednesday the Thirty-first Day of May 1738,

Collation: No title; p. 665 [1]. A. B. C. H. L. N. P. S. W.

The American Antiquarian Society's copy is torn.

1738.

[Royal Arms.] | An Act, | Passed by the Great and General Court or Assembly of His Majesty's Province of the Massachu- | setts-Bay in New-England, Begun and Held at Boston, upon Wednesday the Thirty-first Day | of May, 1738.

Colophon: Boston: | Printed by John Draper, Printer to His Excellency the | Governour and Council. [1738.]

Collation: No title; pp. (9). P. S.

An Act apportioning and assessing a Tax of Thirteen Thousand pounds in Bills of Credit of the new Form and Tenor. The Massachusetts State Library copy has the last page mutilated. "There are two pages each numbered 2, 3, and 4, respectively. The other three are not numbered" (Hildeburn).

1739.

[Royal Arms.] | Acts and Laws | Passed by the Great and General Court or Assembly of His Majesty's Pro- | vince of the Massachusetts-Bay in New-England, Begun and Held at Boston, | upon Wednesday the Thirty-first Day of May 1738. And continued by | Prorogations unto Wednesday the Twenty-ninth Day of November fol- | lowing.

Colophon: Boston: | Printed by John Draper, Printer to His Excellency the Governour | and Council. [1739.]

Collation: No title; pp. 667–684. A. B. C. H. L. N. P. S. W.

1739.

[Royal Arms.] | Acts and Laws | Passed by the Great and General Court or Assembly of His Majesty's Pro- | vince of the Massachusetts-Bay in New England, Begun and Held at Boston, | upon Wednesday the Thirtieth Day of May, 1739.

Colophon: Boston: Printed by John Draper, Printer to His | Excellency the Governour and Council. [1739.]

Collation: No title; pp. 685–691 [1]. A. B. H. L. N. P. S. W.

1740.

[Royal Arms.] | Acts and Laws | Passed by the Great and General Court or Assembly of His Majesty's Pro- | vince of the Massachusetts-Bay in New-England, Begun and Held at Boston, | upon Wednesday the Thirtieth Day of May 1739. And continued by | Prorogations to Wednesday the Fifth Day of December following.

Colophon: Boston: Printed by John Draper, Printer to His | Excellency the Governour and Council. [1740.]

Collation: No title; pp. 693–698. A. B. H. L. N. P. S. W.

1740.

[Royal Arms.] | Acts and Laws | Passed by the Great and General Court or Assembly of His Majesty's Pro- | vince of the Massachusetts-Bay in New-England, Begun and Held at Boston, | upon Wednesday the Thirtieth Day of May 1739. And continued by | Prorogations to Wednesday the Twelfth Day of March following.

Colophon: Boston: Printed by J. Draper, Printer to His Excellency the | Governour and Council. 1740.

Collation: No title; pp. 699, 700. B. H. L. N. P. S. W.

The New York Historical Society's copy is mutilated.

1740.

[Royal Arms.] | Acts and Laws | Passed by the Great and General Court or Assembly of His Majesty's Pro- | vince of the Massachusetts Bay in New-England, begun and held at

Boston, | upon Wednesday the Twenty-eighth Day of May 1740.

Colophon: Boston: Printed by J. Draper, Printer to His | Excellency the Governour and Council. 1740.

Collation: No title; pp. 701–714. B. H. P. S. W.

1740.

[Royal Arms.] | An Act | Passed by the Great and General Court or Assembly of His Majesty's Province of the Massachusetts- | Bay in New-England; Begun and Held at Boston, upon Wednesday the Twenty-eighth Day of | May, 1740.

Colophon: Boston: | Printed by John Draper, Printer to His Excellency the | Governour and Council. 1740.

Collation: No title; pp. (9). P. S.

An Act for apportioning and assessing a Tax of Twenty-four thousand Pounds in Bills of Credit.

1740.

[Royal Arms.] | Acts and Laws | Passed by the Great and General Court or Assembly of His Majesty's Province | of the Massachusetts-Bay in New England, begun and held at Boston | upon Wednesday the Twenty-eighth Day of May, 1740. and continued by Pro- | rogation unto Wednesday the Twentieth Day of August following.

Colophon: Boston: Printed by John Draper, Printer to | His Excellency the Governour & Council. [1740.]

Collation: No title; pp. 715, 716. H. P. S. W.

1740.

[Royal Arms.] | Acts and Laws | Passed by the Great and General Court or Assembly of His Majesty's Pro- | vince of the Massachusetts-Bay in New-England, Begun and Held at

Boston, | upon Wednesday the Twenty-eighth Day of May 1740. And continued | by Prorogations to Wednesday the Nineteenth Day of November following.

Colophon: Boston: Printed by J. Draper, Printer to His Excellency the Gover- | nour and Council. 1740.

Collation: No title; pp. 715–720. B. P. S. W.

"The third session of 1740–41, not issued till January, 1740–41. The paging is misprinted, 715–720 for 717–722, and the error was not corrected until the second session of 1741–42" (Hildeburn).

1741.

[Royal Arms.] | Acts and Laws | Passed by the Great and General Court or Assembly of the Province | of the Massachusetts-Bay in New-England, begun and held at Boston, | upon Wednesday the Twenty-eighth Day of May 1740. And | continued by several Prorogations unto Wednesday the Twenty-sixth | Day of March following.

Collation: No title; pp. 721–728. P. B. S. W.

1741.

[Royal Arms.] | Acts and Laws | Passed by the Great and General Court or Assembly of His Majesty's Pro- | vince of the Massachusetts-Bay in New-England, begun and held at | Boston, upon Wednesday the Eighth Day of July 1741. |

Colophon: Boston: | Printed by J. Draper, Printer to His Excellency | the Governour and Council. [1741.]

Collation: No title; pp. 729–735 [1]. P. S. W.

"The first session of 1741–42, see the next but one preceding for an error in paging, which is continued" (Hildeburn).

1741.

In the House of Representatives, | October 8. 1741. | Voted, | That the Treasurer be directed to ap- | portion the Tax of Nine Thousand Pounds | for the present Year, upon the several | Towns, agreable to the Tax Act which was | issued the last Year. | Sent up for Concurrence, | J. Hobson, Speaker. | In Council, Octo. 8. 1741. | Read and Concur'd. J. Willard, Secr. | Consented to, | W. Shirley. | Copy examin'd, | per J. Willard, Secr.

Collation: 1 leaf. S.

1741.

[Royal Arms.] | Extract | of | An Act | Passed by the Great and General Court or Assembly of His Majesty's Province of the | Massachusetts-Bay in New-England, begun and held at Boston, upon Wednesday the | Twenty-sixth Day of May 1736. And continued by several Prorogations unto | Wednesday the Twenty-fourth Day of November following, and then met. | Entitled, | An Act for supplying the Treasury with the Sum of Eighteen | Thousand Pounds in Bills of Credit of the present Form and | Tenour; and Nine Thousand Pounds in Bills of Credit of a | new Form, etc.

Colophon: Boston: | Printed by J. Draper, Printer to His | Excellency the Governour & Council. 1741.

Collation: No title; pp. (7). S.

1742.

[Royal Arms.] | Acts and Laws, | Passed by the Great and General Court or Assembly of the Province of the | Massachusetts-Bay in New-England: Begun and Held at Boston on Wednesday | the eighth of July 1741. and continued by Prorogation and Adjournment | to Wednesday the sixteenth of September following.

Colophon: Boston: Printed by Samuel Kneeland and Timothy Green, | by Order of His Excellency the Governour, Council and | House of Representatives. MDCCXLII.

Collation: No title; pp. 737–742. P. S. W.

1741.

[Royal Arms.] | An Act | Passed by the Great and General Court or Assembly of His Majesty's Province of the | Massachusetts-Bay in New-England, begun and held at Boston, upon Wednesday the | Eighth Day of July 1741. And continued by Prorogation and Adjournment unto | Wednesday the sixteenth Day of September following.

Colophon: Boston: Printed by J. Draper, Printer to His Excellency the | Governour and Council. [1741.]

Collation: No title; pp. (2). P.

An Act for Inquiry into the rateable Estate of this Province.

1742.

Temporary | Acts and Laws | Of His Majesty's | Province | of the | Massachusetts-Bay | in | New-England. | [Royal Arms.]

Boston, N. E. | Printed and Sold by Samuel Kneeland and Timothy Green, | by Order of His Excellency the Governour, Council and House of Representatives. MDCCXLII.

Collation: Title, 1 p.; Authorization, 1 p.; Table (to p. 74), pp. 4; Table (to p. 205), pp. 1–4; Text, pp. 1–74.

A. B. C. H. HL. L. P. S. W.

The American Antiquarian Society's copy lacks Table to p. 205. The Boston Public Library copy lacks Table to p. 74. The Harvard College Library copy lacks Table to p. 74. The Harvard Law School Library copy lacks Table to p. 205. The Massachusetts State Library copy lacks Table to p. 74.[1]

1742.

[Royal Arms.] | Acts and Laws | Passed by the Great and General Court or Assembly of His Majesty's Province | of the Massachusetts-Bay in New-England, begun and held at Boston, upon | Wednesday the Eighth Day of July 1741.

[1] This volume, when complete, extends to p. 455.

and continued by Prorogation | and Adjournments to Wednesday the Twenty-fifth of November following.

Colophon: Boston: Printed by Samuel Kneeland and Timothy Green, | by Order of His Excellency the Governour Council and | House of Representatives. MDCCXLII.

Collation: No title; pp. 745–757 [1]. P. S. W.

In some copies pp. 746, 747, are misnumbered 176, 177. "The third session of 1741–42. The error in the pagination made in the third session of 1740–41 is corrected by dropping pp. 743–744" (Hildeburn).

1742.

[Royal Arms.] | Acts and Laws, | Passed by the Great and General Court or Assembly of the Province of the | Massachusetts-Bay in New-England: Begun and Held at Boston on Wed- | nesday the eighth of July 1741, and continued by Prorogation and Ad- | journments to Wednesday the seventeenth of March following.

Colophon: Boston: Printed by Samuel Kneeland and Timothy Green, | by Order of His Excellency the Governour Council and House | of Representatives. MDCCXLII.

Collation: No title; pp. 759–766. L. P. S. W.

The Lenox Library copy lacks pp. 763–766.

1742.

[Royal Arms.] | Acts and Laws, | Passed by the Great and General Court or Assembly of the Province of the | Massachusetts-Bay in New England: Begun and held at Boston on Wednes- | day the Twenty-sixth of May 1742.

Colophon: Boston: Printed by Samuel Kneeland and Timothy Green, | by Order of His Excellency the Governour, Council and House | of Representatives. M,DCC,XLII.

Collation: No title; pp. 767–789 [1]. B. L. P. S. W.

The Boston Public Library copy lacks pp. 767–770, 785–789. The Lenox Library copy lacks pp. 767–770, 775–778. The Massachusetts State Library copy has p. 789 slightly torn.

1742.

[Temporary.] [Royal Arms.] | Acts and Laws, | Passed by the Great and General Court or Assembly of His Majesty's Province | of the Massachusetts-Bay in New England: Begun and Held at Boston upon | Wednesday the twenty sixth Day of May 1742. And continued by | Adjournments and Prorogations unto Thursday the Eighteenth of November | following.

Collation: No title; pp. 57–74. A. B. C. H. L. P. S. W.

Issued with pp. 1-56.

1742.

[Royal Arms.] | An Act. | Passed by the Great and General Court or Assembly of the Province of the Massachusetts-Bay in | New-England: Begun and held at Boston on Wednesday the twenty-sixth of May, 1742, and | continued by Adjournment and Prorogation to Thursday the eighteenth of November following.

Colophon: Boston: | Printed by J. Draper, Printer to His | Excellency the Governour, and | Council.

Collation: No title; pp. (10). S.

An Act for apportioning and assessing a Tax of Twenty thousand Pounds.

1742.

Acts | and | Laws, | Of His Majesty's | Province | of the | Massachusetts-Bay | in | New-England. | [Royal Arms.]

Boston in New-England: | Printed and Sold by Samuel Kneeland and Timothy Green, | by Order of His Excellency the Governour, Council and | House of Representatives. MDCCXLII.

Collation: Title to Charter, 1 leaf; Charter, pp. 1–12; Explanatory Charter; pp. 13, 14; Table (to p. 337), pp. 1–28; Title to Acts, 1 p.; Authorization, 1 p.; Acts, pp. 1–333 [1]. A. B. C. H. L. M. N. P. S. W.

Title to Charter reads:

The | Charter | Granted by their Majesties | King William | and Queen Mary, | to the

| Inhabitants | of the | Province | of the Massachusetts-Bay | in | New-England. | Boston in New-England: Printed and Sold by Samuel Kneeland and Timothy Green, | by Order of His Excellency the Governour, Council and | House of Representatives. MDCCXLII.[1]

1743.

[Royal Arms.] | Acts and Laws, | Passed by the Great and General Court or Assembly of His Majesty's Province | of the Massachusetts-Bay in New-England: Begun and Held at Boston upon | Wednesday the twenty-sixth Day of May 1742. And continued by Ad- | journments and Prorogations unto Thursday the thirty first of March following.

Colophon: Boston, N. E. | Printed and Sold by Samuel Kneeland and Timothy Green, by Order | of His Excellency the Governour, Council and House of | Representatives. MDCCXLIII.

Collation: No title; pp. 335–337 [1].

A. B. C. H. L. M. N. P. S. W.

1743.

[Temporary.] [Royal Arms.] | An Act, | Passed by the Great and General Court or Assembly of His Majesty's Province | of the Massachusetts-Bay in New-England: Begun and Held at Boston upon | Wednesday the twenty sixth Day of May 1742. And continued by Ad- | journments and Prorogations unto Thursday the thirty first of March following.

Colophon: Boston, N. E. | Printed and Sold by Samuel Kneeland and Timothy Green, by Order | of His Excellency the Governour, Council, and House of | Representatives. MDCCXLIII.

Collation: No title; pp. 75, 76. A. B. C. HL. L. P. S. W.

1743.

A Bill Intituled, | An Act in Explanation of sundry Acts of | this Province relating to the Payment of | private Debts

[1] This volume, when complete, extends to p. 526.

contracted before the thirty | first Day of October, One Thousand seven | Hundred and forty one.

Collation: No title; pp. (3). L.

The text of the Bill fills pp. 1, 2; on p. 3 is printed the Speech to both Houses of Assembly of W. Shirley, April 23, 1743. Shirley says: "[The Bill] requires a longer Advisement upon it than the Time will allow me, before I am obliged to dismiss you: But I will advise upon the Matter by next May Session, and will then let you know my Sentiments upon it."

1743.

[Royal Arms.] | An Act, | Passed by the Great and General Court or Assembly of His Majesty's Province | of the Massachusetts-Bay in New-England: Begun and Held at Boston upon | Wednesday the twenty fifth Day of May 1743.

Colophon: Boston, N. E. | Printed and Sold by Samuel Kneeland and Timothy Green, by Order | of His Excellency the Governour, Council and House of | Representatives. MDCCXLIII.

Collation: No title; pp. 339, 340.
A. B. C. H. L. M. N. P. S. W.

1743.

[Temporary.] [Royal Arms.] | Acts and Laws, | Passed by the Great and General Court or Assembly of His Majesty's Province | of the Massachusetts-Bay in New-England: Begun and Held at Boston upon | Wednesday the twenty-fifth Day of May 1743.

Colophon: Boston, N. E. | Printed and Sold by Samuel Kneeland and Timothy Green, by Order | of His Excellency the Governour, Council, and House of | Representatives. MDCCXLIII.

Collation: No title; pp. 77–81 [1]. A. B. C. H. L. P. S. W.

1743.

[Royal Arms.] | An Act. | Passed by the Great and General Court or Assembly of the Province of the Massachusetts-

Bay | in New-England: Begun and held at Boston on Wednesday the Twenty fifth of May, 1743.

Colophon: Boston: | Printed by J. Draper, Printer to His | Excellency the Governou[r and] | Council. 1743.

Collation: No title; pp. 10. S.

An Act for apportioning and assessing a Tax of Twenty Thousand Pounds. The Massachusetts State Library copy has the last leaf torn.

1743.

[Royal Arms.] | An Act | Passed by the Great and General Court or Assembly of His Majesty's Province | of the Massachusetts-Bay in New-England: Begun and Held at Boston upon | Wednesday the twenty-fifth Day of May 1743, and continued by Ad- | journment to Thursday the Eighth Day of September following.

Colophon: Boston: N. E. | Printed and Sold by Samuel Kneeland and Timothy Green, by | Order of His Excellency the Governour, Council and House | of Representatives. MDCCXLIII.

Collation: No title; pp. 341–344.

A. B. C. H. L. M. N. P. S. W.

1743.

[Temporary.] [Royal Arms.] | An Act | Passed by the Great and General Court or Assembly of His Majesty's Province | of the Massachusetts-Bay in New-England: Begun and held at Boston upon | Wednesday the twenty-fifth Day of May 1743, and continued by Ad- | journment to Thursday the eighth Day of September following.

Collation: No title; p. 83 [1]. C. L. P. S. W.

1743.

[Temporary.] [Royal Arms.] | Acts and Laws | Passed by the Great and General Court or Assembly of His Majesty's Province | of the Massachusetts-Bay in New-England: Begun and Held at Boston upon | Wednesday the twenty-fifth Day of May 1743, and continued by Ad- | journment to Thursday the eighth Day of September following.

Colophon: Boston: N. E. | Printed and Sold by Samuel Kneeland and Timothy Green, by | Order of His Excellency the Governour, Council, and House | of Representatives. MDCCXLIII.

Collation: No title; pp. 83–89 [1].

A. B. H. L. P. S. W.

1743.

[Royal Arms.] | An Act | Passed by the Great and General Court or Assembly of His Majesty's Province | of the Massachusetts-Bay in New-England: Begun and Held at Boston upon | Wednesday the twenty-fifth Day of May 1743, and continued by Adjourn- | ment and Prorogation to Thursday the twentieth of October following.

Colophon: Boston: N. E. | Printed and Sold by Samuel Kneeland and Timothy Green, by Order | of His Excellency the Governour, Council and House of | Representatives. MDCCXLIII.

Collation: No title; pp. 345–348.

A. B. C. H. L. M. N. P. S. W.

1743.

[Temporary.] [Royal Arms.] | Acts and Laws | Passed by the Great and General Court or Assembly of His Majesty's Province | of the Massachusetts-Bay in New-England: Begun and Held at Boston upon | Wednesday the twenty-fifth Day of May 1743, and continued by Adjourn- | ment and Prorogation to Thursday the twentieth of October following.

Colophon: Boston: N. E. | Printed and Sold by Samuel Kneeland and Timothy Green, by Order | of His Excellency the Governour, Council and House of | Representatives. MDCCXLIII.

Collation: No title; pp. 91–97 [1]. A. B. C. H. L. P. S. W.

1744.

[Royal Arms.] | Acts and Laws | Passed by the Great and General Court or Assembly of His Majesty's Province | of the Massachusetts-Bay in New-England: Begun and held at Boston upon | Wednesday the twenty-fifth Day of May 1743, and continued by Adjourn- | ment and Prorogations to Wednesday the eighth Day of February following.

Colophon: Boston: N. E. | Printed and Sold by Samuel Kneeland and Timothy Green, by Order | of His Excellency the Governour, Council and House of | Representatives. MDCCXLIII.

Collation: No title; pp. 349–352.

A. B. C. H. L. M. N. P. S. W.

1744.

[Royal Arms.] | Acts and Laws | Passed by the Great and General Court or Assembly of His Majesty's Province | of the Massachusetts-Bay in New-England: Begun and Held at Boston upon | Wednesday the twenty-fifth Day of May 1734, and continued by Adjourn- | ment and Prorogations to Wednesday the eighth Day of February following.

Colophon: Boston: | Printed and Sold by Samuel Kneeland and Timothy Green, by Order | of His Excellency the Governour, Council and House of | Representatives. MDCCXLIII.

Collation: No title; pp. 353–356.

A. B. C. H. L. M. N. P. S. W.

1744.

[Temporary.] [Royal Arms.] | An Act | Passed by the Great and General Court or Assembly of His Majesty's Province | of the Massachusetts-Bay in New-England: Begun and held at Boston upon | Wednesday the twenty-fifth Day of May 1743, and continued by Adjourn- | ment and Prorogations to Wednesday the eighth Day of February following.

Colophon: Boston: N. E. | Printed and Sold by Samuel Kneeland and Timothy Green, by Order | of His Excellency the Governour, Council and House of | Representatives. MDCCXLIII. [1743–4.]

Collation: No title; pp. 99–109 [1]. A. B. C. H. L. P. S. W.

1744.

[Temporary.] [Royal Arms.] An Act | Passed by the Great and General Court or Assembly of His Majesty's Province | of the Massachusetts-Bay in New-England: Begun and held at Boston upon | Wednesday the twenty-fifth Day of June 1743, and continued by Adjourn- | ment and Progations to Wednesday the eighth Day of February following.

Collation: No title; pp. 99–101 [1]. L. W.

This is a separate edition of Chapter vii, the text being identical with pp. 99–101 of the preceding item.

1744.

[Temporary.] [Royal Arms.] | Acts and Laws | Passed by the Great and General Court or Assembly of His Majesty's Province | of the Massachusetts-Bay in New-England: Begun and held at Boston, upon | Wednesday the thirtieth Day of May 1744.

Colophon: Boston: | Printed and Sold by Samuel Kneeland and Timothy Green, by Order | of his Excellency the Governour Council and House of | Representatives. MDCCXLIV.

Collation: No title; pp. 111–124. A. B. C. H. L. P. S. W.

1744.

[Royal Arms.] | An Act | Passed by the Great and General Court or Assembly of the Province of the Massachusetts- | Bay in New-England, begun and held at Boston, on Wednesday the Thirtieth Day of | May 1744.

Colophon: Boston: N. E. | Printed by John Draper, Printer to His Excellency the | Governour and Council. 1744.

Collation: No title; pp. (10). S.

An Act for apportioning and assessing a Tax of Twenty-five Thousand Pounds.

1744.

[Royal Arms.] | An Act | Passed by the Great and General Court or Assembly of His Majesty's Province | of the Massachusetts-Bay in New England: Begun and Held at Boston upon | Wednesday the thirtieth Day of May 1744, and continued by Adjournment | to Thursday the ninth Day of August following.

Colophon: Boston: Printed by Samuel Kneeland and Timothy Green, | by Order of His Excellency the Governour, Council and House of | Representatives. MDCCXLIV.

Collation: No title; pp. 357–359 [1].
A. B. C. H. L. M. N. P. S. W.

1744.

[Temporary.] [Royal Arms.] | Acts and Laws | Passed by the Great and General Court or Assembly of His Majesty's Province | of the Massachusetts-Bay in New-England: Begun and Held at Boston upon | Wednesday the thirtieth Day of May 1744, and continued by Adjournment | to Thursday the ninth Day of August following.

Colophon: Boston: Printed by Samuel Kneeland and Timothy Green, | by Order of His Excellency the Governour, Council and House of | Representatives. MDCCXLIV.

Collation: No title; pp. 125–127 [1].
A. B. C. H. L. P. S. W.

1744.

[Royal Arms.] | An Act, | Passed by the Great and General Court or Assembly of His Majesty's Province | of the

Massachusetts-Bay in New-England: Begun and Held at Boston upon | Wednesday the thirtieth Day of May 1744, and continued by Adjournment | and Prorogations to the tenth Day of October following.

Colophon: Boston: Printed by Samuel Kneeland and Timothy Green, | by Order of His Excellency the Governour, Council and House of | Representatives. MDCCXLIV.

Collation: No title; pp. 361, 362.

A. B C. H. L. M. N. P. S. W.

1744.

[Temporary.] [Royal Arms.] | Acts and Laws, | Passed by the Great and General Court or Assembly of His Majesty's Province | of the Massachusetts-Bay in New-England: Begun and Held at Boston upon | Wednesday the thirtieth Day of May 1744, and continued by Adjournment | and Prorogations to the tenth Day of October following.

Colophon: Boston: Printed by Samuel Kneeland and Timothy Green, | by Order of His Excellency the Governour, Council and House of | Representatives. MDCCXLIV.

Collation: No title; pp. 229 [129]–135 [1].

A. B. C. H. L. P. S. W.

Pages 129–132 are misnumbered 229–232.

1745.

[Royal Arms.] | Acts and Laws, | Passed by the great and General Court or Assembly of His Majesty's Province | of the Massachusetts-Bay in New-England: Begun and held at Boston upon | Wednesday the thirtieth Day of May 1744, and continued by Adjourn- | ment and Prorogations to Wednesday the twenty-eighth Day of November | following.

Colophon: Boston: Printed by Samuel Kneeland and Timothy Green, | by Order of His Excellency the Governour, Council, and House | of Representatives. 1745.

Collation: No title; pp. 363–366.

A. B C. H. L. M. N. P. S. W

1745.

[Temporary.] [Royal Arms.] | Acts and Laws, | Passed by the Great and General Court or Assembly of His Majesty's Province | of the Massachusetts-Bay in New-England: Begun and held at Boston upon | Wednesday the thirtieth Day of May 1744, and continued by Adjourn- | ment and Prorogations to Wednesday the twenty-eighth Day of November | following.

Colophon: Boston: Printed by Samuel Kneeland and Timothy Green, | by Order of His Excellency the Governour, Council, and House | of Representatives. 1745.

Collation: No title; pp. 137–158. A. B. C. H. L. P. S. W.

1745.

[Royal Arms.] | An Act | passed by the Great and General Court or Assembly of the Province of the Massachusetts- | Bay in New-England: Begun and held at Boston on Wednesday the Twenty-fifth Day | of May, 1745.

Colophon: Boston: Printed by John Draper, Printer to His | Excellency the Governour and Council. 1745.

Collation: No title; pp. 8 [12]. S.

An Act for apportioning and assessing a Tax of Thirty Thousand Pounds. In the caption the date "Twenty-fifth" is a misprint for "Twenty-ninth."

1745.

[Temporary.] [Royal Arms.] | Acts and Laws, | Passed by the Great and General Court or Assembly of His Majesty's Province | of the Massachusetts-Bay in New-England: Begun and Held at Boston upon | Wednesday the twenty-ninth Day of May 1745.

Colophon: Boston: Printed and Sold by Samuel Kneeland and Timothy | Green, by Order of His Excellency the Governour, Council and | House of Representatives. MDCCXLV.

Collation: No title; pp. 159–171[1]. A. B. C. H. L. P. S. W.

1745.

[Temporary.] [Royal Arms.] | Acts and Laws | Passed by the Great and General Court or Assembly of His Majesty's Province | of the Massachusetts-Bay in New-England: Begun and Held at Boston upon | Wednesday the twenty ninth Day of May 1745. And continued by Ad- | journment to Wednesday the seventeenth Day of July following.

Colophon: Boston: Printed and Sold by Samuel Kneeland and Timothy | Green, by Order of His Excellency the Governour, Council and | House of Representatives. MDCCXLV.

Collation: No title; pp. 173–176. A. B. C. H. L. P. S. W.

1745.

[Temporary.] [Royal Arms.] | An Act | Passed by the Great and General Court or Assembly of His Majesty's Province | of the Massachusetts-Bay in New-England: Begun and held at Boston upon | Wednesday the twenty ninth-Day of May 1745. And continued by | Adjournments and Prorogations to Wednesday the thirtieth Day of October | following.

Collation: No title; p. 177 [1]. A. B. C. H. L. P. S. W.

1745.

[Royal Arms.] | Acts and Laws | Passed by the Great and General Court or Assembly of His Majesty's Province | of the Massachusetts-Bay in New-England: Begun and held at Boston upon | Wednesday the twenty ninth-Day of May 1745. And continued by | Adjournments and Prorogations to Wednesday the eleventh Day of December | following.

Colophon: Boston: N. E. Printed and Sold by Samuel Kneeland and | Timothy Green, by Order of His Excellency the Governour, | Council and House of Representatives. MDCCXLV.

Collation: No title; pp. 367–372.
A. B. C. H. L. M. N. P. S. W.

1745.

[Royal Arms.] | An Act | Passed by the Great and General Court or Assembly of the Province of the | Massachusetts-Bay in New-England; begun and held at Boston, | upon Wednesday the Twenty-ninth Day of May, 1745, and continued by | Prorogations to Wednesday the Eleventh Day of December following.

Collation: No title; pp. 1–4. L.

An Act for granting unto His Majesty several Rates and Duties of Import and Tunnage of Shipping. The Lenox Library copy is imperfect, lacking one or more pages, as p. 4 has the word "And" at the bottom.

1746.

[Temporary.] [Royal Arms.] | Acts and Laws | Passed by the Great and General Court or Assembly of His Majesty's Province | of the Massachusetts-Bay in New England: Begun and held at Boston upon | Wednesday the twenty-ninth Day of May 1745. And continued by | Adjournments and Prorogations to Wednesday the eleventh Day of December | following.

Colophon: Boston: N. E. Printed and Sold by Samuel Kneeland and | Timothy Green, by Order of His Excellency the Governour, | Council and House of Representatives. MDCCXLVI.

Collation: No title; pp. 179–190. A. B. C. H. L. P. S. W.

The Boston Athenæum copy has the date in the Colophon misprinted MDCCLXV.

1746.

[Temporary.] [Royal Arms.] | Acts and Laws | Passed by the Great and General Court or Assembly of His Majesty's Province | of the Massachusetts-Bay in New England: Begun and Held at Boston upon | Wednesday the twenty-eighth Day of May 1746.

Colophon: Boston: Printed by Samuel Kneeland and Timothy Green, | by Order of His Excellency the Governour, Council and House | of Representatives. MDCCXLVI.

Collation: No title; pp. 191–201[1]. A. B. C. H. L. P. S. W.

1746.

[Royal Arms.] | An Act | Passed by the Great and General Court or Assembly of the Province of the Massachusetts- | Bay in New-England: Begun and held at Boston on Wednesday the Twenty-eighth Day | of May 1746.

Colophon: Boston: Printed by J. Draper, Printer to His Excellency the Governor & Council.

Collation: No title; pp. 7 [11]. S.

An Act for apportioning and assessing a Tax of Twenty-eight Thousand Four Hundred and Ninety-nine Pounds Seven Shillings and Six Pence.

1746.

[Temporary.] [Royal Arms.] | An Act | Passed by the Great and General Court or Assembly of His Majesty's Province | of the Massachusetts-Bay in New-England: Begun and held at Boston upon | Wednesday the twenty-eighth of May 1746. And continued by Adjourn- | ments to Monday the fourth of August following.

Colophon: Boston: | Printed and Sold by S. Kneeland and T. Green, by Order of the | Governour, Council and Representatives. MDCCXLVI.

Collation: No title; pp. 203–205 [1]. A. B. C. H. L. P. S. W.

1746.

[Temporary.] [Royal Arms.] | Acts and Laws | Passed by the Great and General Court or Assembly of His Majesty's Province | of the Massachusetts-Bay in New-England: Begun and held at Boston upon | Wednesday the twenty-eighth of May 1746. And continued by Adjourn- | ments to Wednesday the twenty-seventh of August following.

Colophon: Boston: | Printed and Sold by S. Kneeland and T. Green, by Order of the | Governour, Council and Representatives. MDCCXLVI.

Collation: No title; pp. 207–214. A. B. C. H. L. P. S. W.

1746.

[Royal Arms.] | An Act | Passed by the Great and General Court or Assembly of His Majesty's Province | of the Massachusetts-Bay in New-England: Begun and held at Boston upon | Wednesday the twenty-eighth of May 1746. And continued by Adjourn- | ments to Thursday the sixth of November following.

Colophon: Boston: | Printed and Sold by S. Kneeland and T. Green, by Order of the | Governour, Council and Representatives. MDCCXLVI.

Collation: No title; pp. 373, 374.
A. B. C. H. L. M. N. P. S. W.

1746.

[Temporary.] [Royal Arms.] | An Act | Passed by the Great and General Court or Assembly of His Majesty's Province | of the Massachusetts-Bay in New-England: Begun and held at Boston, upon | Wednesday the twenty-eighth of May 1746. And continued by Adjourn- | ments to Thursday the sixth of November following.

Colophon: Boston: | Printed and Sold by S. Kneeland and T. Green, by Order of the | Governour, Council and Representatives. MDCCXLVI.

Collation: No title; pp. 215–218. A. B. C. H. L. P. S. W.

1746

[Temporary.] [Royal Arms.] | Acts and Laws | Passed by the Great and General Court or Assembly of His Majesty's

Pro- | vince of the Massachusetts-Bay in New-England: Begun and held at | Boston upon Wednesday the twenty-eighth Day of May 1746. And con- | tinued by Adjournments to Wednesday the twenty fourth Day of Decem- | ber following.

Colophon: Boston: N. E. | Printed and Sold by S. Kneeland and T. Green, by Order of the | Governour, Council and Representatives. MDCCXLVI.

Collation: No title; pp. 219–228. A. B. C. H. L. P. S. W.

1747.

[Temporary.] [Royal Arms.] | Acts and Laws, | Passed by the Great and General Court or Assembly of His Majesty's Province | of the Massachusetts-Bay in New-England: Begun and Held at Boston, upon | Wednesday the twenty-eighth Day of May 1746, and continued by | Adjournments to Thursday the sixteenth Day of April following.

Colophon: Boston: N. E. | Printed and Sold by Samuel Kneeland and Timothy Green, by Order | of the Governour, Council and Representatives. | MDCCXLVII.

Collation: No title; 229–241 [1]. A. B. C. H. L. P. S. W.

1747.

[Temporary.] [Royal Arms.] | Acts and Laws, | Passed by the Great and General Court or Assembly of His Majesty's Province | of the Massachusetts-Bay in New-England: Begun and held at Boston upon | Wednesday the twenty-seventh Day of May 1747.

Colophon: Boston: N. E. Printed and Sold by Samuel Kneeland and | Timothy Green, by Order of the Governour, Council and | House of Representatives. MDCCXLVII.

Collation: No title; pp. 243–249 [1]. A. B. C. H. L. P. S. W.

1747.

[Royal Arms.] | An Act | passed by the Great and General Court or Assembly of the Province of the Massachusetts- | Bay in New-England: Begun and Held at Boston on Wednesday the Twenty-seventh | Day of May 1747.

Colophon: Boston: New-England: | Printed by John Draper, Printer to His Excellency the Governour and Council. | 1747.

Collation: No title; pp. 8 [12]. P. S.

An Act for apportioning and Assessing a Tax of Thirty-nine Thousand One hundred and Three Pounds Thirteen Shillings and Seven Pence.

1747.

[Temporary.] [Royal Arms.] | Acts and Laws | Passed by the Great and General Court or Assembly of His Majesty's Province | of the Massachusetts-Bay in New-England: Begun and Held at Boston upon | Wednesday the twenty-seventh Day of May 1747, and continued by | Adjournments to Wednesday the twelfth Day of August following.

Colophon: Boston: N. E. | Printed and Sold by Samuel Kneeland and Timothy Green, by | Order of His Excellency the Governour, Council and House | of Representatives. MDCCXLVII.

Collation: No title; pp. 251–254. A. B. C. H. L. P. S. W.

1747.

[Royal Arms.] | Acts and Laws | Passed by the Great and General Court or Assembly of His Majesty's Province | of the Massachusetts-Bay in New-England: Begun and Held at Boston upon | Wednesday the twenty-seventh Day of May 1747, and continued by | Adjournments to Wednesday the twelfth Day of August following.

Colophon: Boston: N. E. Printed and Sold by S. Kneeland and T. Green, | by Order of His Excellency the Governour, Council and | House of Representatives. MDCCXLVII.

Collation: No title; pp. 375–377 [1].
A. B. C. H. L. M. N. P. S. W.

1747.

[Temporary.] [Royal Arms.] | An Act | Passed by the Great and General Court or Assembly of His Majesty's Province | *of the Massachusetts-Bay in New England: Begun* and held at Boston upon | Wednesday the twenty-seventh Day of May 1747, and continued by | Adjournments and Prorogation to Wednesday the fourteenth Day of October | following.

Colophon: Boston: N. E. | Printed and Sold by Samuel Kneeland and Timothy Green, by | Order of the Governour, Council and House of Represen- | tatives. MDCCXLVII.

Collation: No title; pp. 255–258. A. B. C. H. L. P. S. W.

1748.

[Royal Arms.] | Acts and Laws, | Passed by the Great and General Court or Assembly of His Majesty's Province | of the Massachusetts-Bay in New-England: Begun and Held at Boston upon | Wednesday the twenty-seventh Day of May 1747, and continued by | Adjournments and Prorogations to Wednesday the third Day of February | following.

Colophon: Boston: N. E. | Printed and Sold by S. Kneeland and T. Green, by Order of the | Governour, Council, and House of Representatives. | MDCCXLVII.

Collation: No title; pp. 379, 380.
A. B. C. H. L. M. N. P. S. W.

1748.

[Temporary.] [Royal Arms.] | An Act | Passed by the Great and General Court or Assembly of His Majesty's Province | of the Massachusetts-Bay in New-England: Begun and held at Boston upon | Wednesday the twenty-seventh Day of May 1747, and continued by | Adjournments and Prorogations to Wednesday the third Day of February | following.

Colophon: Boston: N. E. | Printed and Sold by S. Kneeland and T. Green, by Order of the | Governour, Council, and House of Representatives. | MDCCXLVIII.

Collation: No title; pp. 259–261 [1]. A. B. C. H. L. P. S. W.

1748.

[Temporary.] [Royal Arms.] | Acts and Laws | Passed by the Great and General Court or Assembly of His Majesty's Province | of the Massachusetts-Bay in New-England: Begun and held at Boston upon | Wednesday the twenty-fifth Day of May 1748.

Colophon: Boston: | Printed and Sold by S. Kneeland and T. Green, by | Order of His Excellency the Governour, Council, and House of | Representatives. MDCCXLVIII.

Collation: No title; pp. 263–274. A. B. C. H. L. P. S. W.

1748.

[Royal Arms.] | An Act | Passed by the Great and General Court or Assembly of the Province of the Massachusetts- | Bay in New-England: Begun and Held at Boston, on Wednesday the Twenty-fifth |Day of May 1748.

Colophon: Boston: New-England: | Printed by John Draper, Printer to His Excellency the Governour and Council. | 1748.

Collation: No title; pp. 8 [12]. S.

An Act for apportioning and assessing a Tax of Ninety-one Thousand Pounds.

1748.

[Temporary.] [Royal Arms.] | Acts and Laws | Passed by the Great and General Court or Assembly of His Majesty's Pro- | vince of the Massachusetts-Bay in New-England: Begun and held at | Boston upon Wednesday the twenty-fifth

Day of May 1748, and con- | tinued by Prorogations to Wednesday the twenty-sixth Day of October | following, and then met.

Colophon: Boston: N. E. Printed and Sold by S. Kneeland and T. Green, | by Order of His Excellency the Governour, Council and House | of Representatives. MDCCXLVIII.

Collation: No title; pp. 275–277 [1].

A. B. C. H. L. P. S. W.

1748.

[Temporary.] [Royal Arms.] | Acts and Laws | Passed by the Great and General Court or Assembly of His Majesty's Pro- | vince of the Massachusetts-Bay in New-England: Begun and held at Boston | upon Wednesday the twenty-fifth Day of May 1748, and continued by | Prorogation and Adjournments to Wednesday the twenty-first Day of | December following, and then met.

Colophon: Boston: Printed and Sold by S. Kneeland and T. Green, | by Order of His Excellency the Governour, Council and House | of Representatives. MDCCXLVIII.

Collation: No title; pp. 279–283 [1].

A. B. C. H. L. P. S. W.

1748.

[Royal Arms.] | An Act | Passed by the Great and General Court or Assembly of His Majesty's Pro- |vince of the Massachusetts-Bay in New-England: Begun and held at Boston | upon Wednesday the twenty-fifth Day of May 1748, and continued by | Prorogation and Adjournments to Wednesday the twenty-first Day of | December following, and then met.

Colophon: Boston: Printed and Sold by S. Kneeland and T. Green, by | Order of His Excellency the Governour, Council and House of | Representatives. MDCCXLVIII.

Collation: No title; pp. 381 386. A. B. M.

1749.

[Royal Arms.] | Acts and Laws | Passed by the Great and General Court or Assembly of His Majesty's Pro- | vince of the Massachusetts-Bay in New-England: Begun and held at Boston | upon Wednesday the twenty-fifth Day of May 1748, and continued by | Prorogation and Adjournments to Wednesday the twenty-first Day of | December following, and then met.

Colophon: Boston: N. E. Printed and Sold by S. Kneeland and T. Green, | by Order of his Excellency the Governour, Council, and House | of Representatives. MDCCXCIX.

Collation: No title; pp. 381–390.

A. B. C. H. L. M. N. P. S. W.

In some copies, the caption on p. 381 reads "An Act Passed," etc.

1749.

Province of the | Massachusetts-Bay, | [Royal Arms.] | Extract of two Clauses or Paragraphs from | An Act | Passed by the Great and General Court or Assembly of His Majesty's Province of the Massachusetts- | Bay in New-England; Begun and held at Boston upon Wednesday the Twenty-fifth Day of May 1748, and continued by | Prorogation and Adjournments to Wednesday the Twenty-first Day of December following, and then met; Entitled, An Act | for drawing in the Bills of Credit of the several Denominations which have at any Time been issued by this Government and | are still outstanding, and for ascertaining the Rate of coin'd Silver in this Province for the future.

Colophon: Boston: Printed by John Draper, Printer to His Excellency the Governour and Council. [1749.]

Collation: No title; pp. 4. P. S.

The Massachusetts State Library copy has the date 1749 written in manuscript above the Royal Arms. The copy is torn.

1749.

[Temporary.] [Royal Arms.] | Acts and Laws | Passed by the Great and General Court or Assembly of His Majesty's Pro- | vince of the Massachusetts-Bay in New-England: Begun and held at | Boston upon Wednesday the twenty-fifth Day of May 1748, and con- | tinued by Prorogation and Adjournments to Wednesday the fifth Day of | April following, and then met.

Colophon: Boston: N. E. Printed and Sold by S. Kneeland and T. Green, | by Order of His Excellency the Governour, Council, and House | of Representatives. MDCCXLIX.

Collation: No title; pp. 285, 286. A. B. C. H. L. P. S. W.

1749.

[Temporary.] [Royal Arms.] | Acts and Laws | Passed by the Great and General Court or Assembly of His Majesty's Pro- | vince of the Massachusetts-Bay in New-England: Be-gun and held at | Boston upon Wednesday the thirty-first Day of May 1749.

Collation: No title; pp. 287–289. A. B. C. H. L. P. S. W.

1749.

[Temporary.] Acts and Laws | Passed by the Great and General Court or Assembly of His Majesty's | Province of the Massachusetts-Bay in New-England; begun and held at | Boston upon Wednesday the thirty-first Day of May 1749, and conti- | nued by Prorogation to Wednesday the second Day of August follow- | ing, and then met.

Colophon: Boston: | Printed and Sold by S. Kneeland and T. Green, by Order of the | Governour, Council and Representatives. MDCCXLIX.

Collation: No title; pp. 290–295 [1]. A. B. C. H. L. P. S. W.

1749.

[Royal Arms.] | Acts and Laws | Passed by the Great and General Court or Assembly of his Majesty's Pro- | vince of the Massachusetts-Bay in New-England: Begun and held at | Boston upon Wednesday the thirty-first Day of May 1749. and conti- | nued by sundry Prorogations to the twenty-third of November follow- | ing, and then met.

Colophon: Boston: Printed and Sold by S. Kneeland and T. Green, | by Order of His Honour the Lieutenant Governour, Council | and House of Representatives. MDCCXLIX.

Collation: No title; pp. 391–394.

A. B. C. H. L. M. N. P. S. W.

1749.

[Temporary.] [Royal Arms.] | Acts and Laws | Passed by the Great and General Court or Assembly of His Majesty's Pro- | vince of the Massachusetts-Bay in New-England: Begun and held at | Boston upon Wednesday the thirty-first Day of May 1749. and conti- | nued by sundry Prorogations to the twenty-second of November follow- | ing, and then met.

Colophon: Boston: Printed and Sold by S. Kneeland and T. Green, | by Order of His Honour the Lieutenant Governour, Council | and House of Representatives. MDCCXLIX.

Collation: No title; pp. 297–306. A. B. C. H. L. P. S. W.

1750.

[Royal Arms.] | Acts and Laws | Passed by the Great and General Court or Assembly of His Majesty's Pro- | vince of the Massachusetts-Bay in New-England: Begun and held at | Boston upon Wednesday the thirty-first Day of May 1749, and conti- | nued by sundry Prorogations and an Adjournment to the twenty-second | Day of March following, and then met.

Colophon: Boston: N. E. Printed and Sold by S. Kneeland and T. | Green, by Order of His Excellency the Governour, Council | and House of Representatives. MDCCL.

Collation: No title; pp. 395–398.

A. B. C. H. L. M. N. P. S. W.

1750.

[Temporary.] [Royal Arms.] | Acts and Laws | Passed by the Great and General Court or Assembly of His Majesty's Pro- | vince of the Massachusetts-Bay in New-England: Begun and held at | Boston upon Wednesday the thirty-first Day of May 1749, and conti- | nued by sundry Prorogations and an Adjournment to the twenty-second | Day of February following, and then met.

Colophon: Boston: N. E. Printed and Sold by S. Kneeland and T. | Green, by Order of His Excellency the Governour, Council | and House of Representatives. MDCCL.

Collation: No title; pp. 307–315 [1].

A. B. C. H. L. P. S. W.

In the caption, February has been corrected in manuscript to March.

1750.

[Royal Arms.] | An Act | Passed by the Great and General Court or Assembly of His Majesty's Pro- | vince of the Massachusetts-Bay in New-England: Begun and Held at | Boston upon Wednesday the thirtieth Day of May 1750, and continued | by Prorogations to Wednesday the twenty-sixth of September following.

Colophon: Boston: Printed and Sold by S. Kneeland and | T. Green, by Order of His Honour the Lieutenant | Governour, Council and House of Representatives. 1750.

Collation: No title; p. 399 [1]. A. B. H. L. M. N. P. S. W.

1750.

[Temporary.] [Royal Arms.] | Acts and Laws | Passed by the Great and General Court or Assembly of His Majesty's

Pro- | vince of the Massachusetts-Bay in New-England: Begun and held | at Boston upon Wednesday the thirtieth Day of May 1750.

Colophon: Boston: N. E. Printed and Sold by S. Kneeland and | T. Green, by Order of His Honour the Lieutenant Governour, | Council and House of Representatives. MDCCL.

Collation: No title; pp. 317–322. A. B. C. H. L. P. S. W.

1750.

[Temporary.] [Royal Arms.] | Acts and Laws | Passed by the Great and General Court or Assembly of His Majesty's Pro- | vince of the Massachusetts-Bay in New England: Begun and Held at | Boston upon Wednesday the thirtieth Day of May 1750, and continued | by Prorogations to Wednesday the twenty-sixth of September following.

Collation: No title; pp. 333 [323]–342 [332].
A. B. C. H. L. P. S. W.

In some copies, p. 326 is correctly numbered. There are two copies in the Boston Public Library. One has by mistake p. 399 of the Acts and Laws of 1742 printed on the same sheet with pp. 341 [331], 342 [332].

1750.

[Temporary.] [Royal Arms.] | Acts and Laws | Passed by the Great and General Court or Assembly of His Majesty's | Province of the Massachusetts-Bay in New-England: Begun and Held | at Boston upon Wednesday the thirtieth Day of May 1750; and con- | tinued by Prorogations to Thursday the tenth of January following.

Colophon: Boston: Printed and Sold by S. Kneeland and | T. Green, by Order of His Honour the Lieutenant- | Governour, Council and House of Representatives. 1750.

Collation: No title; pp. 333–341 [1]. A. B. H. L. P. S. W.

1750.

[Royal Arms.] | An Act Passed by the Great and General Court or Assembly of His Majesty's Province of the Massachusetts-Bay in New-England: Begun and Held at Boston upon Wednesday the thirtieth Day of May 1750, and continued by Prorogations to Thursday the tenth of January following. An Act for preventing and suppressing of Riots, Routs, and unlawful assemblies.

Boston: Printed by Order of His Honour the Lieutenant-Governour, Council, and House of Representatives. 1750.

Collation: No title; 1 p. A. B. C. H. L. P. S. W.

This item is Chapter xii, printed on pp. 339, 340, of the Temporary Laws.

1751.

A | Patent | for | Plymouth | in | New=England. | To which is annexed, | Extracts from the Records of that Colony, &c. &c.

Boston; New-England: Printed by John Draper. | 1751.

Collation: Title, 1 leaf; New-Plymouth Patent, pp. 1–7; Certification, p. 8; Extracts From the Plymouth Records, pp. 9–19; Authorization, p. (20). A. H. M.

The Boston Athenæum copy has Title torn.

1751.

[Royal Arms.] | Acts and Laws | Passed by the Great and General Court or Assembly of his Majesty's | Province of the Massachusetts-Bay in New-England: Begun and Held | at Boston upon Wednesday the thirtieth Day of May 1750; and con- | tinued by Prorogations to Thursday the tenth of January following.

Colophon: Boston: Printed and Sold by S. Kneeland and | T. Green, by Order of His Honour the Lieutenant- | Governour, Council and House of Representatives. 1750.

Collation: No title; pp. 401–404.

A. B. C. H. L. M. N. P. S. W.

1751.

[Royal Arms.] | Acts and Laws | Passed by the Great and General Court or Assembly of His Majesty's | Province of the Massachusetts-Bay in New-England: Begun and Held | at Boston upon Wednesday the thirtieth Day of May 1750; and con- | tinued by Prorogations and Adjournment to Wednesday the twenty- | seventh Day of March following.

Colophon: Boston: Printed and Sold by S. Kneeland and | T. Green, by Order of His Honour the Lieutenant- | Governour, Council & House of Representatives. 1751.

Collation: No title; pp. 405–410.
A. B. C. H. L. M. N. P. S. W.

1751.

[Temporary.] [Royal Arms.] | Acts and Laws | Passed by the Great and General Court or Assembly of His Majesty's | Province of the Massachusetts-Bay in New-England: Begun and Held | at Boston upon Wednesday the thirtieth Day of May 1750; and con- | tinued by Prorogations and Adjournment to Wednesday the twenty- | seventh Day of March following.

Colophon: Boston: Printed and Sold by S. Kneeland and | T. Green, by Order of His Honour the Lieutenant- | Governour, Council & House of Representatives. 1751.

Collation: No title; pp. 343–346. A. B. H. L. P. S. W.

1751.

[Royal Arms.] | Acts and Laws | Passed by the Great and General Court or Assembly of His Majesty's | Province of the Massachusetts-Bay in New-England: Begun and Held | at Boston upon Wednesday the twenty-ninth Day of May, 1751.

Colophon: Boston: Printed and Sold by S. Kneeland and | T. Green, by Order of His Honour the Lieutenant- | Governour, Council & House of Representatives, 1751.

Collation: No title; pp. 411–414.

A. B. C. H. L. M. N. P. S. W.

1751.

[Temporary.] [Royal Arms.] Acts and Laws | Passed by the Great and General Court or Assembly of His Majesty's | Province of the Massachusetts-Bay in New-England: Begun and Held | at Boston upon Wednesday the twenty-ninth Day of May 1751.

Colophon: Boston: Printed and Sold by S. Kneeland and | T. Green, by Order of His Honour the Lieutenant- | Governour, Council, & House of Representatives. 1751.

Collation: No title; pp. 347–354.

A. B. H. H[L]. L. P. S. W.

The Harvard College Library copy lacks pp. 351–354.

1751.

[Royal Arms.] | An Act | Passed by the Great and General Court of the Province of the Massachusetts- | Bay in New-England: Begun and Held at Boston, on Wednesday the Twenty-ninth | Day of May, 1751.

Colophon: New-[ ] | Printed by John Draper, Printer to His Honou[r] | M,DCC,LI

Collation: No title; pp. 7 [11]. S.

An Act for apportioning and assessing a Tax of Thirty thousand three hundred and ninety-four Pounds eight Shillings and eight Pence. The Massachusetts State Library copy has the first leaf and the last two leaves badly torn.

1751.

[Temporary.] [Royal Arms.] | An Act | Passed by the Great and General Court or Assembly of His Majesty's Province | of the Massachusetts-Bay in New-England: Begun and Held at Boston | upon Wednesday the twenty-ninth Day of May 1751, and continued by | Prorogation to Wednesday the second Day of October following.

Colophon: Boston: Printed and Sold by S. Kneeland and T. Green, by | Order of His Honour the Lieut. Governour, Council and House of | Representatives. 1751.

Collation: No title; p. 355 [1]. A. B. H^{L}. P. S. W.

1751.

[Royal Arms.] | At the Parliament begun and holden at Westminster, the | Tenth Day of November, Anno Dom. 1747, in the | Twenty first Year of the Reign of our Sovereign Lord | George the Second, by the Grace of God, of | Great Britain, France and Ireland, King, Defender | of the Faith, &c. | And from thence continued by several Prorogations to the Seventeenth Day | of January, 1750, being the Fourth Session of this present Parliament.

Colophon: Boston: Printed and Sold by S. Kneeland and | T. Green, by Order of His Honour the Lieutenant | Governour, Council and House of Representatives. 1751.

Collation: No title; pp. 415–420.
A. B. C. H. L. N. P. S. W.

An Act for Regulating the Commencement of the Year; and for Correcting the Callender now in Use.

1752.

[Royal Arms.] | Acts and Laws, | Passed by the Great and General Court or Assembly of His Majesty's Province | of the Massachusetts-Bay in New-England: Begun and Held at Boston | upon Wednesday the twenty-ninth Day of May 1751, and continued by | Prorogations to Friday the twenty-seventh Day of December following.

Colophon: Boston: Printed and Sold by S. Kneeland and | T. Green, by Order of His Honour the Lieutenant | Governour, Council and House of Representatives. 1752.

Collation: No title; pp. 421–424. A. B. H. L. N. P. S. W.

1752.

[Temporary.] [Royal Arms.] | Acts and Laws, | Passed by the Great and General Court or Assembly of His Majesty's Province | of the Massachusetts-Bay in New-England: Begun and Held at Boston | upon Wednesday the twenty-ninth Day of May 1751, and continued by | Prorogations to Friday the twenty-seventh Day of December following.

Colophon: Boston: Printed and Sold by S. Kneeland and | T. Green, by Order of His Honour the Lieutenant | Governour, Council and House of Representatives. 1752.

Collation: No title; pp. 357–362. A. B. H^{L}. P. S. W.

1752.

[Royal Arms.] | Acts and Laws | Passed by the Great and General Court or Assembly of His Majesty's Pro- | vince of the Massachusetts-Bay in New-England: Begun and Held at | Concord in the County of Middlesex, upon Wednesday the twenty-seventh | Day of May, 1752.

Colophon: Boston: Printed and Sold by S. Kneeland and | T. Green, by Order of His Honour the Lieutenant | Governour, Council and House of Representatives. 1752.

Collation: No title; pp. 425, 426. B. C. H. L. N. P. S. W.

1752.

[Temporary.] [Royal Arms.] | Acts and Laws, | Passed by the Great and General Court or Assembly of His Majesty's | Province of the Massachusetts-Bay in New-England: Begun and Held | at Concord in the County of Middlesex, upon Wednesday the twenty- | seventh Day of May, 1752.

Colophon: Boston: Printed and Sold by S. Kneeland and | T. Green, by Order of His Honour the Lieutenant- | Governour, Council & House of Representatives, 1752.

Collation: No title; pp. 363–370. A. B. H^{L}. L. P. S. W.

1752.

[Royal Arms.] | An Act | Passed by the Great and General Court or Assembly of the Province of the Massachusetts- | Bay in New-England: Begun and Held at Concord, on Wednesday the Twenty- | seventh Day of May, 1752.

Colophon: Boston; New-England: | Printed by John Draper, Printer to His Honour the Lieutenant- | Governour and Council. 1752.

Collation: No title; pp. 8 [12]. S.

An Act for the Supply of the Treasury with Eight thousand one hundred and forty-two Pounds, four Shillings.

1752.

[Royal Arms.] | At the Parliament begun and holden at Westminster, the Tenth Day of November, Anno Dom. 1747, in | the Twenty first Year of the Reign of our Sovereign | Lord George the Second, by the Grace of God, | of Great Britain, France and Ireland, King, De- | fender of the Faith, &c. | And from thence continued by several Prorogations to the Fourteenth | Day of November, 1751, being the Fifth Session of the present | Parliament.

Colophon: Boston: Printed and Sold by S. Kneeland and | T. Green, by Order of His Honour the Lieutenant Go- | vernour, Council and House of Representatives. 1752.

Collation: No title; pp. 427–430. A. B. C. H. L. N. P. S. W.

An Act relating to the Attestation of Wills and Codicils, concerning Real Estate, *etc.*

1752.

[Temporary.] [Royal Arms.] | Acts and Laws, | Passed by the Great and General Court or Assembly of His Majesty's | Province of the Massachusetts-Bay in New-England: Begun and Held | at Concord in the County of Middlesex, upon Wednesday the twenty- | seventh Day of May 1752. And continued by Prorogations to Wed- | nesday the twenty-second Day of November following, and then met | at Cambridge.

Colophon: Boston: Printed and Sold by S. Kneeland and | T. Green, by Order of His Honour the Lieutenant Go- | vernour, Council and House of Representatives. 1752.

Collation: No title; pp. 371–382. A. B. H^L^. L. P. S. W.

1753.

[Royal Arms.] | Acts and Laws, | Passed by the Great and General Court or Assembly of His Majesty's | Province of the Massachusetts-Bay in New-England: Begun and Held | at Concord in the County of Middlesex, upon Wednesday the twenty- | seventh Day of May 1752. And continued by Prorogations to Wed- | nesday the twenty-second Day of November following, and then met | at Cambridge.

Colophon: Boston: Printed and Sold by S. Kneeland and | T. Green, by Order of His Honour the Lieutenant Go- | vernour, Council and House of Representatives. 1753.

Collation: No title; pp. 431, 432. A. B. C. H. L. N. P. S. W.

1753.

[Royal Arms.] | Acts and Laws, | Passed by the Great and General Court or Assembly of His Majesty's | Province of the Massachusetts-Bay in New-England: Begun and Held | at Concord in the County of Middlesex, upon Wednesday the twenty- | seventh Day of May 1752. And continued by Prorogations and | Adjournment, to Wednesday the twenty-eighth of March following, | and then met at Boston.

Colophon: Boston: Printed and Sold by S. Kneeland and | T. Green, by Order of His Honour the Lieutenant Go- | vernour, Council and House of Representatives. 1753.

Collation: No title; pp. 433–438. A. B. C. H. L. N. P. S. W.

1753.

[Temporary.] [Royal Arms.] | An Act, | Passed by the Great and General Court or Assembly of His Majesty's | Province of the Massachusetts-Bay in New-England: Begun and Held | at Concord in the County of Middlesex, upon Wednesday the twenty- | seventh Day of May 1752. And continued by Prorogations and | Adjournment, to Wednesday the twenty-eighth Day of March following, | and then met at Boston.

Colophon: Boston: Printed and Sold by S. Kneeland and | T. Green, by Order of His Honour the Lieutenant Go- | vernour, Council and House of Representatives. 1753.

Collation: No title; pp. 383–389 [1]. A. B. H[L]. L. P. S. W.

1753.

[Royal Arms.] | Acts and Laws, | Passed by the Great and General Court or Assembly of His Majesty's Pro- | vince of the Massachusetts-Bay in New-England: Begun and Held at Boston | in the County of Suffolk, upon Wednesday the thirtieth Day of | May, 1753. |

Colophon: Boston: Printed and Sold by S. Kneeland and T. | Green, by Order of His Honour the Lieut. Governour, | Council and House of Representatives. 1753.

Collation: No title; pp. 439–443 [1].

A. B. C. H. L. N. P. S. W.

The Lenox Library has two copies of pp. 441, 442. In one, the headline on p. 442 is "Firing of Woods;" in the other, it has been corrected to "Greenfield a District."

1753.

[Temporary.] [Royal Arms.] | Acts and Laws, | Passed by the Great and General Court or Assembly of His Majesty's Pro- | vince of the Massachusetts-Bay in New-England: Begun and held at Boston | in the County of Suffolk, upon Wednesday the Thirtieth Day of | May, 1753.

Colophon: Boston: Printed and Sold by S. Kneeland and T. | Green, by Order of His Honour the Lieut. Governour, | Council and House of Representatives. 1753.

Collation: No title; pp. 391–400. A. B. HL. L. P. S. W.

1753.

[Royal Arms.] | An Act | Passed by the Great and General Court or Assembly of the Province of the Massachusetts- | Bay in New-England; Begun and Held at Boston, on Wednesday the Thirtieth | Day of May 1753.

Colophon: Boston; New-England: | Printed by John Draper, Printer to His Honour the Lieutenant- | Governour and Council, 1753.

Collation: No title; pp. 8 [12]. P. S.

An Act for the supply of the Treasury with Nine Thousand Pounds. In the Massachusetts State Library copy, the Colophon reads, "Boston in New-England:" *etc.*

1753.

[Royal Arms.] | An Act, | Passed by the Great and General Court or Assembly of His Majesty's | Province of the Massachusetts-Bay in New-England: Begun and held | at Boston, in the County of Suffolk, upon Wednesday the thirtieth Day | of May 1753. and continued by Prorogations to Wednesday the fifth | Day of September following, and then met.

Colophon: Boston: Printed and Sold by S. Kneeland and | T. Green, by Order of the Governour, Council and | House of Representatives. 1753.

Collation: No title; pp. 445, 446. A. B. C. H. L. N. P. S. W.

1753.

[Temporary.] [Royal Arms.] | Acts and Laws, | Passed by the Great and General Court or Assembly of His Majesty's |

Province of the Massachusetts-Bay, in New-England: Begun and held | at Boston, in the County of Suffolk, upon Wednesday the thirtieth Day | of May 1753. and continued by Prorogations to Wednesday the fifth | Day of September following, and then met.

Colophon: Boston: Printed and Sold by S. Kneeland and | T. Green, by Order of the Governour, Council and | House of Representatives. 1753.

Collation: No title; pp. 401–403 [1]. A. B. L. P. S.

1754.

[Temporary.] [Royal Arms.] | Acts and Laws, | Passed by the Great and General Court or Assembly of His Majesty's | Province of the Massachusetts-Bay in New-England: Begun and held at | Boston, in the County of Suffolk, upon the thirtieth Day of May 1753, and from | thence continued by Prorogations to Tuesday the fourth Day of Decem- | ber, 1753.

Colophon: Boston: Printed and Sold by S. Kneeland and T. Green, | by Order of the Governour, Council and House of Representatives. | 1754.

Collation: No title; pp. 405–414. A. B. P. S.

The Boston Athenæum copy lacks pp. 409–414. The Pennsylvania Historical Society's copy lacks pp. 405–409, 413, 414. These pages have the date 1754 in the headline and contain Chapters ix–xvi, all of which "Acts were Published January 26. 1754."

1754.

An Act for preventing Mischief by unruly Dogs on the Islands of Martha's-Vineyard, Chebaquiduck, and also on the Island of Nantucket.

Collation: No title; p. 415 [1]. A. P.

This page has the date 1753 in the headline, and contains Chapter xvii, which "Pass'd at the Session of the General Court in December 1753." The page was issued with pp. 417–424.

1754.

[Royal Arms.] | Acts and Laws, | Passed by the Great and General Court or Assembly of His Majesty's | Province of the Massachusetts-Bay in New-England: Begun and held at | Boston in the County of Suffolk, upon the thirtieth of May 1753, and from | thence continued by Prorogations to Tuesday the fourth Day of Decem- | ber, 1753.

Colophon: Boston: Printed and Sold by S. Kneeland and T. Green, by Order of His | Excellency the Governour, Council and House of Representatives. 1754.

Collation: No title; pp. 447–452. A. B. C. H. L. N. P. S. W.

1754.

[Royal Arms.] | Acts and Laws, | Passed by the Great and General Court or Assembly of His Majesty's | Province of the Massachusetts-Bay in New-England: Begun and held | at Boston, in the County of Suffolk, upon Wednesday the thirtieth Day | of May 1753, and continued by Prorogations to Wednesday the twenty- | seventh Day of March following, and then met. |

Collation: No title; pp. 453–460. A. B. H. L. N. P. S. W.

1754.

[Temporary.] [Royal Arms.] | Acts and Laws, | Passed by the Great and General Court or Assembly of His Majesty's | Province of the Massachusetts-Bay, in New-England: Begun and held | at Boston, in the County of Suffolk, upon Wednesday the thirtieth Day | of May 1753, and continued by Prorogations to Wednesday the twenty- | seventh Day of March following, and then met.

Collation: No title; pp. 417–424. A. P.

The Boston Athenæum copy lacks pp. 421–424.

1754.

[Royal Arms.] | Acts and Laws | Passed by the Great and General Court or Assembly of His Majesty's | Province of the Massachusetts-Bay in New-England: Begun and held | at Boston, in the County of Suffolk, upon Wednesday the twenty-ninth | Day of May 1754.

Collation: No title; pp. 461, 462. A. B. H. L. N. P. S. W.

1754.

[Temporary.] [Royal Arms.] | Acts and Laws | Passed by the Great and General Court or Assembly of His Majesty's | Province of the Massachusetts-Bay, in New-England: Begun and held | at Boston, in the County of Suffolk, upon Wednesday the twenty-ninth | Day of May 1754.

Collation: No title; pp. 425–431 [1]. L. P.

1754.

[Royal Arms.] | An Act | Passed by the Great and General Court or Assembly of the Province of the Massachusetts- | Bay in New-England: Begun and Held at Boston, on Wednesday the Twenty- | ninth Day of May 1754.

Colophon: Boston; in New-England: | Printed by John Draper, Printer to His Excellency the Governour | and Council. 1754.

Collation: No title; pp. 8 [12]. S.

An Act for the Supply of the Treasury with the Sum of Nine Thousand four Hundred fifty-six Pounds seven Shillings and eight Pence.

1754.

[Royal Arms.] | Acts and Laws | Passed by the Great and General Court or Assembly of His Ma- | jesty's Province of the Massachusetts-Bay in New-England: Be- | gun and held at Boston upon Wednesday the Twenty-ninth | Day of May

1754. And continued by Adjournment unto | Thursday the seventeenth Day of October following.

Collation: No title; pp. 463–467 [1].

A. B. C. H. L. N. P. S. W.

The Boston Public Library copy has p. 467 mutilated.

1754.

[Temporary.] [Royal Arms.] | An Act | Passed by the Great and General Court or Assembly of His Majesty's | Province of the Massachusetts-Bay in New-England: Begun and Held | at Boston in the County of Suffolk, upon Wednesday the Twenty- | ninth Day of May 1754, and continued by Adjournment to | Thursday the nineteenth Day of October following.

Collation: No title; pp. 433, 434. L. P.

1754.

[Temporary.] [Royal Arms.] | An Act | Passed by the Great and General Court or Assembly of His Ma- | jesty's Province of the Massachusetts-Bay in New-England: Be-gun and Held at Boston upon Wednesday the twenty-ninth Day of | May 1754. And continued by Adjournment unto Thursday | the nineteenth Day of October following.

Colophon: Boston: N. E. | Printed by S. Kneeland, by Order of the Governour, | Council and House of Representatives. 1754.

Collation: No title; pp. 435–442. B. L. P. S. W.

The American Antiquarian Society's copy lacks pp. 439–442.

1754.

[Temporary.] [Royal Arms.] | Acts and Laws | Passed by the Great and General Court or Assembly of His Ma- | jesty's Province of the Massachusetts-Bay in New-England: Be- | gun and held at Boston upon Wednesday the twenty-ninth | Day of May 1754. And continued by Adjournment unto | Thursday the seventeenth Day of October following.

Collation: No title; pp. 443–452. B. L. P. S.

The Massachusetts State Library copy has pp. 451, 452, torn.

1755.

[Temporary.] [Royal Arms.] | An Act, | Passed by the Great and General Court or Assembly of His Ma- | jesty's Province of the Massachusetts-Bay in New-England: Be- | gun and held at Boston upon Wednesday the twenty-ninth | Day of May 1754. And continued by Adjournment and Prorogation unto Wednesday the fifth Day of February | following.

Colophon: Boston: | Printed | by S. Kneeland by Order of the Governour, Council | and House of Representatives. 1755.

Collation: No title; pp. 453–455. P.

1755.

[Royal Arms.] | An Act | Passed by the Great and General Court or Assembly of His Ma- | jesty's Province of the Massachusetts-Bay in New-England: Be- | gun and Held at Boston upon Wednesday the twenty-ninth | Day of May, 1754, and continued by sundry Prorogations | unto Tuesday the twenty-fifth Day of March following.

Collation: No title; pp. 469, 470. A. B. H. L. N. P. S. W.

1755.

[Royal Arms.] | An Act | Passed by the Great and General Court or Assembly of His Ma- | jesty's Province of the Massachusetts-Bay in New-England: Be- | gun and Held at Boston upon Wednesday the twenty-eighth Day of May, 1755.

Collation: No title; p. 471 [1]. A. B. H. L. N. P. S.

1755.

Temporary Acts and Laws | Of His Majesty's | Province | of the | Massachusetts-Bay | in | New-England. | [Royal Arms.]

Boston, N. E. | Printed by Order of His Excellency the Governour, | Council and House of Representatives: | And Sold by S. Kneeland in Queen-Street. | 1755

Collation: Title, 1 p.; Authorization, 1 p.; Table, pp. 1–8; Laws, pp. 1–166. B. H. L. P. S. W.

The Harvard College Library copy lacks Table, pp. 5–8. The Massachusetts State Library copy lacks Table, which is in manuscript.[1]

1755.

[Temporary.] [Royal Arms.] | Acts and Laws | Passed by the Great and General Court or Assembly of His Ma- | jesty's Province of the Massachusetts-Bay in New-England: Be- | gun and Held at Boston upon Wednesday the twenty-eighth | Day of May 1755.

Collation: No title; pp. 167–174. B. H. L. P. S. W.

Contains Chapters i–vii.

1755.

[Temporary.] [Royal Arms.] | An Act, | Passed by the Great and General Court or Assembly of His Ma- | jesty's Province of the Massachusetts-Bay in New-England: Be- | gun and Held at Boston upon Wednesday the twenty-eighth | Day of May 1755.

Collation: No title; pp. 167, 168. L.

An Act for the more effectual Prevention of Supplies of Provisions, and War-like Stores to the French, from any Parts of this Province. This is headed Chapter i. It is the same as Chapter iii of the preceding item.

---

[1] This volume, when complete, extends to p. 550.

1755.

[Royal Arms.] | An Act | Passed by the Great and General Court or Assembly of the Province of the | Massachusetts-Bay in New-England: Begun and Held at Boston, on | Wednesday the Twenty-eighth Day of May 1755.

Colophon: Boston; New-England: | Printed by John Draper, Printer to His Excellency the Governour and | the Honourable His Majesty's Council. 1755

Collation: No title; pp. 8 [12]. P. S.

An Act for the Supply of the Treasury, *etc.*

1755.

[Temporary.] [Royal Arms.] | An Act | Passed by the Great and General Court or Assembly of His Ma- | jesty's Province of the Massachusetts-Bay in New-England: | Begun and Held at Boston upon Wednesday the twenty-eighth | Day of May 1755, and continued by Prorogation to Wednes- | day the sixth Day of August following.

Collation: No title; pp. 175, 176. B. H. L. P. S. W.

1755.

[Temporary.] [Royal Arms.] | Acts and Laws | Passed by the Great and General Court or Assembly of His Ma- | jesty's Province of the Massachusetts-Bay in New-England; | specially convened at Boston upon Friday the fifth Day of Sep- | tember 1755.

Colophon: Boston: | Printed by S. Kneeland, by Order of His Honour the Lieut. | Governour, Council and House of Representatives. 1755.

Collation: No title; pp. 177–180. B. H. L. P. S. W.

Contains Chapters ix–xi.

1755.

[Temporary.] [Royal Arms.] | An Act | Passed by the Great and General Court or Assembly of His Ma- | jesty's Province of the Massachusetts-Bay in New-England; | specially convened at Boston, on Friday the fifth Day of Sep- | tember 1755.

Colophon: Boston, N. E. | Printed by S. Kneeland, by Order of His Honour the | Lieutenant Governour, Council and House of Represen- | tatives. 1755.

Collation: No title; pp. 177, 178. L.

An Act for the more speedy levying of Soldiers for the Expedition against Crown-Point. This is Chapter xi of the preceding item.

1755.

[Royal Arms.] | An Act | Passed by the Great and General Court or Assembly of His Majesty's Province of | the Massachusetts-Bay in New-England; specially convened at Boston, upon | Friday the Fifth Day of September 1755.

Colophon: Boston: Printed by John Draper, Printer to His Honour the Lieutenant- | Governour and Council. 1755.

Collation: No title; pp. 5. P. S.

An Act for apportioning and assessing a Tax of Eighteen Thousand Pounds.

1755.

[Royal Arms.] | An Act | Passed by the Great and General Court or Assembly of His Ma- | jesty's Province of the Massachusetts-Bay in New-England: Be- | gun and Held at Boston upon Wednesday the twenty-eighth | Day of May, 1755. And continued by Prorogations to Wed- | nesday the twenty-fourth Day of September following and | then met.

Collation: No title; p. 473 [1]. A. B. H. L. N. P. S.

1755.

[Temporary.] [Royal Arms.] | Acts and Laws | Passed by the Great and General Court or Assembly of His Ma- | jesty's Province of the Massachusetts-Bay in New-England: Be- | gun and Held at Boston upon Wednesday the twenty-eighth | Day of May 1755. And continued by Prorogations to Wed- | nesday the twenty-fourth Day of September following, and | then met.

Colophon: Boston: | Printed by S. Kneeland, by Order of His Honour the Lieut. | Governour, Council and House of Representatives. 1755.

Collation: No title; pp. 181, 182. B. H. L. P. S. W.

1755.

[Temporary.] [Royal Arms.] | Acts and Laws | Passed by the Great and General Court of His Ma- | jesty's Province of the Massachusetts-Bay in New-England: Be- | gun and Held at Boston upon Wednesday the twenty-eighth | Day of May 1755. And continued by Prorogations and Ad- | journment to Wednesday the twenty-second Day of October | following.

Colophon: Boston: | Printed by S. Kneeland, by Order of His Honour the Lieut. | Governour, Council and House of Representatives. 1755.

Collation: No title; pp. 183–186. B. H. L. P. S. W.

1756.

[Temporary.] [Royal Arms.] | An Act | Passed by the Great and General Court or Assembly of His Ma- | jesty's Province of the Massachusetts-Bay in New-England: Be-| gun and Held at Boston upon Wednesday the twenty-eighth | Day of May, 1755. And continued by sundry Prorogations to | Wednesday the Eleventh Day of December following and then | met.

Colophon: Boston: | Printed by S. Kneeland, by Order of His Honour the Lieut. | Governour, Council and House of Representatives. 1755.

Collation: No title; pp. 187, 188. B. H. L. P. S. W.

Some copies have p. 188 misnumbered 176. In the Lenox Library copy, p. 187 is misnumbered.

1756.

[Temporary.] [Royal Arms.] | Acts and Laws, | Passed by the Great and General Court or Assembly of His Ma- | jesty's Province of the Massachusetts-Bay in New-England: Be- | gun and Held at Boston upon Wednesday the twenty-eighth Day | of May, 1755. And continued by sundry Prorogations and | Adjournment to Wednesday the Fourteenth Day of January | following, and then met.

Colophon: Boston: N. E. Printed by S. Kneeland, by Order | of the Governour, Council and House of Represen- | tatives. MDCCLVI.

Collation: No title; pp. 189–220. B. H. L. P. S. W.

1756.

[Royal Arms.] | An Act | For the better recruiting His Majesty's | Forces on the Continent of America; and for the better | Regulation of the Army, and preventing of Desertion therein.

Colophon: Boston; New-England: Re-printed by John Draper, Printer to | His Excellency the Governour and Council.

Collation: No title; pp. 1–4. W.

An Act as to inlisting indented servants: "This Act . . . shall have Continuance for the Space of Three Years, from and after the Twenty-fifth of March, One Thousand Seven Hundred and Fifty-six."

1756.

[Royal Arms.] | An Act, | Passed by the Great and General Court or Assembly of His Ma- | jesty's Province of the Massachusetts-Bay in New-England: Be- | gun and Held at Boston upon Wednesday the twenty-eighth Day | of May, 1755. And continued by sundry Prorogations and | Adjournments to Tuesday the thirtieth Day of March fol- | lowing, and then met.

Colophon: Boston: N. E. Printed by S. Kneeland, by Order | of the Governour, Council and House of Represen- | tatives. MDCCLVI.

Collation: No title; pp. 195,196. L.

An Act for the more speedy levying of Soldiers for the Expedition against Crown-Point. Published April 14, 1756.

1756.

[Royal Arms.] | An Act, | Passed by the Great and General Court or Assembly of His Ma- | jesty's Province of the Massachusetts-Bay in New-England: Be- | gun and Held at Boston upon Wednesday the twenty-eighth Day | of May, 1755. And continued by sundry Prorogations and | Adjournments to Tuesday the thirtieth Day of March fol- | lowing, and then met.

Colophon: Boston: N. E. Printed by S. Kneeland, by Order | of the Governour, Council and House of Represen- | tatives. MDCCLVI.

Collation: No title; pp. 199, 200. L.

An Act in Addition to An Act Intitled, An Act for regulating the Militia. Published April 16, 1756.

1756.

[Temporary.] [Royal Arms.] | Acts and Laws, | Passed by the Great and General Court or Assembly of His Ma- | jesty's Province of the Massachusetts-Bay in New-England: Be- | gun and Held at Boston upon Wednesday the twenty-eighth Day | of May 1755. And continued by sundry Prorogations and | Adjournments to Tuesday the thirtieth Day of March follow- | ing, and then met. |

Colophon: Boston: N. E. | Printed by S. Kneeland, by Order of the Governour, | Council and House of Representatives. MDCCLVI.

Collation: No title; pp. 221–230. B. H. L. P. S. W.

1756.

[Royal Arms.] | An Act | Passed by the Great and General Court or Assembly of the Province | of the Massachusetts-Bay in New-England: Begun and Held at | Boston, on Wednesday the Twenty-eighth Day of May 1755, | and continued by Prorogation and Adjournments to Tuesday | the Thirtieth Day of March following.

Colophon: Boston; New-England: Printed by John Draper, Printer to His Excellency | the Governour and Council. 1756.

Collation: No title; pp. 1–9 [1]. L.

An Act for granting unto His Majesty several Rates and Duties of Impost and Tunnage of Shipping.

1756.

[Temporary.] [Royal Arms.] | Acts and Laws, | Passed by the Great and General Court or Assembly of His Ma-| jesty's Province of the Mussachusetts-Bay in New-England: Be- | gun and Held at Boston upon Wednesday the twenty-sixth Day | of May 1756.

Colophon: Boston: | Printed by S. Kneeland, by Order of his Honour the Lieut. | Governour, Council and House of Representatives. 1756.

Collation: No title; pp. 231–237 [1]. B. H. L. P. S. W.

1756.

[Royal Arms.] | An Act | Passed by the Great and General Court or Assembly of the Province of the | Massachusetts-Bay in New-England: Begun and Held at Boston, on | Wednesday the Twenty-sixth Day of May 1756.

Colophon: Boston; New-England: Printed by John Draper, Printer | to His Honour the Lieutenant-Governour and Council. 1756.

Collation: No title; pp. 7 [11]. S.

An Act for the Supply of the Treasury, *etc.*

1756.

[Temporary.] [Royal Arms.] | Acts and Laws | Passed by the Great and General Court or Assembly of His Ma-| jesty's Province of the Massachusetts-Bay in New-England: Be- | gun and Held at Boston upon Wednesday the twenty-sixth Day | of May 1756. And continued by Prorogations to the Eleventh | Day of August following, and then met.

Colophon: Boston: N. E. | Printed by Samuel Kneeland, by Order of His Excellency | the Governour, Council and House of Represen- | tatives. 1756.

Collation: No title; pp. 239, 240. B. H. L. P. S. W.

1756.

A Bill | Concerning Bankrupts, and for the Relief of Credi- | tors against such Persons as shall become Bank- | rupts.

Collation: No title; pp. 1–4. L.

Read in the House of Representatives August 24, 1756. On August 25 it was "Ordered, That the further Consideration of the Bill be referred to the next Fall Sessions, and that in the mean Time the same be printed."

1756.

[Royal Arms.] | An Act | Passed by the Great and General Court or Assembly of His Ma-| jesty's Province of the Massachusetts-Bay in New-England: Be- | gun and Held at Boston, upon Wednesday the twenty-sixth Day | of May

1756. And continued by Prorogations and Adjourn- | ment, to the fifth Day of October following, and then met. |

Colophon: Boston: N. E. | Printed by Samuel Kneeland, by Order of His Honour the | Lieut. Governour, Council and House of Represen- | tatives. 1766.

Collation: No title; pp. 475, 476. A. B. H. L. N. P. S.

1756.

[Temporary.] [Royal Arms.] | Acts and Laws | Passed by the Great and General Court or Assembly of His Ma- | jesty's Province of the Massachusetts-Bay in New-England: Be- | gun and Held at Boston, upon Wednesday the twenty-sixth Day | of May 1756. And continued by Prorogations and Adjourn- | ment, to the fifth Day of October following, and then met.

Colophon: Boston: N. E. | Printed by Samuel Kneeland, by Order of His Honour the | Lieut. Governour, Council and House of Represen- | tatives. 1756.

Collation: No title; pp. 241–250. B. H. L. P. S. W.

1757.

[Royal Arms.] | Acts and Laws, | Passed by the Great and General Court or Assembly of His Ma- | jesty's Province of the Massachusetts-Bay in New-England: Be- | gun and Held at Boston, upon Wednesday the twenty-sixth Day | of May 1756. And continued by sundry Prorogations, to the | sixth Day of January following, and then met.

Colophon: Boston: | Printed by Samuel Kneeland, by Order of his Honour | the Lieut. Governour, Council and House of Repre- | sentatives. 1757.

Collation: No title; pp. 477–480. A. B. C. H. L. N. P. S.

1757.

[Temporary.] [Royal Arms.] | Acts and Laws, | Passed by the Great and General Court or Assembly of His Ma- | jesty's Province of the Massachusetts-Bay in New-England: Be- | gun and Held at Boston, upon Wednesday the twenty-sixth Day | of May 1756. And continued by sundry Prorogations, to the | sixth Day of January following, and then met.

Colophon: Boston: | Printed by Samuel Kneeland, by Order of His Honour | the Lieut. Governour, Council and House of Represen- | tatives. 1757.

Collation: No title; pp. 251–281 [1]. B. H. L. P. S. W.

In some copies the word Representatives in the Colophon is thus divided: Repre- | sentatives.

1757.

[Royal Arms.] | An Act | Passed by the Great and General Court or Assembly of His Ma- | jesty's Province of the Massachusetts-Bay in New-England: Be- | gun and Held at Boston, upon Wednesday the Twenty-sixth Day | of May 1756. And continued by Prorogations and Ad- | journment, to the fifth Day of October following, and then met.

Collation: No title; pp. 251–253. L.

An Act for the better regulating the Choice of Petit Jurors. Published October 19, 1756. Printed with the next item.

1757.

An Act, | Passed by the Great and General Court or Assembly of His Ma- | jesty's Province of the Massachusetts-Bay in New-England: Be- | gun and Held at Boston, upon Wednesday the twenty-sixth Day | of May 1756. And continued by sundry Prorogations, to the | sixth Day of January following, and then met.

Collation: No title; pp. 253, 254. L.

An Act in Addition to an Act Intitled, An Act for the better regulating the Choice of Petit Jurors. Published January 11, 1757. Printed with the preceding item.

1757.

[Royal Arms.] |An Act, | Passed by the Great and General Court or Assembly of His Ma- | jesty's Province of the Massachusetts-Bay in New-England: Be- | gun and Held at Boston, upon Wednesday the twenty-sixth Day | of May 1756. And continued by sundry Prorogations, to the | sixth Day of January following, and then met.

Colophon: Boston: Printed by S. Kneeland, by Order of his Honour | the Lieut. Governour, Council and House of Representatives.

Collation: No title; pp. 259–261 [1]. L.

An Act for the more speedy levying Eighteen Hundred Men inclusive of Officers, to be employed in his Majesty's Service.

1757.

[Royal Arms.] | An Act, | Passed by the Great and General Court or Assembly of His Ma- | jesty's Province of the Massachusetts-Bay in New-England: Be- | gun and Held at Boston, upon Wednesday the twenty-sixth Day | of May 1756. And continued by sundry Prorogations and | Adjournment, to the thirtieth Day of March following, and | then met.

Colophon: Boston: N. E. | Printed by Order of the Honourable his Majesty's Council, | and House of Representatives. | And Sold by S. Kneeland, in Queen-Street. 1757.

Collation: No title; pp. 491 [481]–493 [483] [1].

A. B. H. L. P. S.

1757.

[Temporary.] [Royal Arms.] | Acts and Laws, | Passed by the Great and General Court or Assembly of His Ma- | jesty's Province of the Massachusetts-Bay in New-England: Be- | gun and Held at Boston, upon Wednesday the twenty-sixth Day | of May 1756. And continued by sundry Prorogations and | Adjournment, to the thirtieth Day of March following, and | then met.

Colophon: Boston. N. E. | Printed by Order of His Majesty's Council and House of | Representatives. And Sold by S. Kneeland | in Queen-Street. 1757.

Collation: No title; pp. 283–292. B. H. L. P. S. W.

1757.

[Royal Arms.] | An Act | Passed by the Great and General Court of His Ma- | jesty's Province of the Massachusetts-Bay in New-England: Be- | gun and Held at Boston, upon Wednesday the twenty-sixth Day | of May 1756. And continued by sundry Prorogations and | Adjournment, to the thirtieth Day of March following, and | then met.

Collation: No title; pp. 286, 287 [1]. L.

An Act to prevent the Desertion of Soldiers during the present War with France. Published April 8, 1757.

1757.

[Royal Arms.] | An Act, | Passed by the Great and General Court or Assembly of His Ma- | jesty's Province of the Massachusetts-Bay in New-England: Be- | gun and Held at Boston, upon Wednesday the twenty-sixth Day | of May 1756. And continued by sundry Prorogations and | Adjournment, to the thirtieth Day of March following, and | then met.

Collation: No title; pp. 289, 290. L.

An Act for Enquiring into the Rateable Estates of the Province.

1757.

[Royal Arms.] | Acts and Laws, | Passed by the Great and General Court or Assembly of His Ma- | jesty's Province of the Massachusetts-Bay in New-England: Be- | gun and Held at Boston upon Wednesday the twenty-fifth Day | of May, 1757.

Colophon: Boston: N. E. Printed by Order of His Majesty's Council, and House | of Representatives. And Sold by S. Kneeland, in Queen-Street.

Collation: No title; pp. 495 [485], 496 [486].
A. B. HL. L. P. S.

1757.

[Temporary.] [Royal Arms.] | Acts and Laws, | Passed by the Great and General Court or Assembly of His Ma- | jesty's Province of the Massachusetts-Bay in New-England: Be- | gun and Held at Boston upon Wednesday the twenty-fifth Day | of May 1757.

Colophon: Boston: N. E. | Printed by Order of His Majesty's Council and House of Repre- | sentatives, 1757. And Sold by S. Kneeland, in Queen-Street.

Collation: No title; pp. 293–300. B. H. L. P. S. W.

1757.

[Royal Arms.] | An Act | Passed by the Great and General Court or Assembly of the Province of the | Massachusetts-Bay in New-England: Begun and Held at Boston on Wed- | nesday the Twenty-fifth Day of May 1757.

Colophon: Boston in New-England: | Printed by John Draper, Printer to the Honourable His Majesty's Council. | 1757.

Collation: No title; pp. 7 [11]. L. P. S.

An Act for apportioning and assessing the sum of Eighty-one Thousand three Hundred and Eighty-six Pounds thirteen Shillings and four Pence.

1757.

[Temporary.] [Royal Arms.] | Acts and Laws, | Passed by the Great and General Court or Assembly of His Ma- | jesty's Province of the Massachusetts-Bay in New-England: | Begun and Held at Boston upon Wednesday the twenty-fifth | Day of May, 1757: And continued by Prorogations to the | sixteenth Day of August following, and then met.

Colophon: Boston: | Printed by Order of His Excellency the Governour, Council | and House of Representatives. And Sold by S. Kneeland | in Queen-Street. 1757.

Collation: No title; pp. 301–318. B. H. L. P. S. W.

1758.

[Royal Arms.] | Acts and Laws | Passed by the Great and General Court or Assembly of His Ma- | jesty's Province of the Massachusetts-Bay in New-England: | Begun and Held at Boston, upon Wednesday the twenty-fifth | Day of May 1757. And continued by Prorogations to Wed- | nesday the twenty-third Day of November following and then met.

Colophon: Boston: N. E. | Printed by S. Kneeland, by Order of His Excellency | the Governour, Council and House of Representatives. | 1758.

Collation: No title; pp. 487–489 [1]. A. B. H. L. P. S.

1758.

[Temporary.] [Royal Arms.] | Acts and Laws | Passed by the Great and General Court or Assembly of His Ma- | jesty's Province of the Massachusetts-Bay in New-England: | Begun and Held at Boston, upon Wednesday the twenty-fifth | Day of May 1757. And continued by Prorogations to Wed- | nesday the twenty-third Day of November following, and | then met.

Colophon: Boston, N. E. | Printed by S. Kneeland, by Order of His Excellency | the Governour, Council and House of Representatives. | 1758.

Collation: No title; pp. 319–339 [1]. B. H. L. P. S. W.

1758.

An Act | Passed by the Great and General Court or Assembly of His Ma- | jesty's Province of the Massachusetts-Bay in New-England: | Begun and held at Boston in New-England, upon Wednesday | the twenty-fifth Day of May Anno Domini, 1757, and conti- | nued by sundry Prorogations to Wednesday the twenty-third | Day of November following, and then met.

Collation: No title; pp. 1–4. L.

An Act in Addition to the several Acts of this Province for Regulating the Militia. Published January 26, 1758.

1758.

[Royal Arms.] | Acts and Laws, | Passed by the Great and General Court or Assembly of His Ma- | jesty's Province of the Massachusetts-Bay in New-England: | Begun and Held at Boston, upon Wednesday the twenty-fifth: | Day of May 1757. And continued by Prorogations to Thurs- | day the second Day of March following, and then met.

Colophon: Boston, N. E. | Printed by S. Kneeland by Order of His Excellency | the Governour, Council, and House of Repre- | sentatives. 1758.

Collation: No title; pp. 491, 492. A. B. H. L. P. S.

The Lenox Library copy is mutilated.

1758.

[Temporary.] [Royal Arms.] | Acts and Laws, | Passed by the Great and General Court or Assembly of His Ma- |

jesty's Province of the Massachusetts-Bay in New-England: | Begun and Held at Boston, upon Wednesday the twenty-fifth | Day of May 1757. And continued by Prorogations to Thurs- | day the second Day of March following, and then met.

Colophon: Boston: Printed by S. Kneeland, by Order of His Ex- | cellency the Governour, Council and House of Representatives. | 1758.

Collation: No title; pp. 341–348. **B. H. L. P. S. W.**

1758.

An Act | Passed by the Great and General Court or Assembly of His Ma- | jesty's Province of the Massachusetts-Bay in New-England: | Begun and Held at Boston, upon Wednesday the twenty-fifth | Day of May 1757. And continued by Prorogations to Thurs- | day the second Day of March following, and then met.

Colophon: Boston: Printed by S. Kneeland, by Order of His Ex- | cellency the Governour, Council and House of Representatives. | 1758.

Collation: No title; p. 1. **L.**

An Act for laying an Embargo upon Ships and other Vessels in this Province.

1758.

[Royal Arms.] | An Act | Passed by the Great and General Court or Assembly of His Ma- | jesty's Province of the Massachusetts-Bay in New-England: Begun and Held at Boston, upon Wednesday the twenty-fifth | Day of May 1757. And continued by Prorogations and Ad- | journment to Tuesday the eighteenth Day of April following, | and then met.

Colophon: Boston: Printed by S. Kneeland, by Order of his Excellency the | Governour, Council, and House of Representatives. 1758.

Collation: No title; p. 493 [1]. **B. H. L. P. S.**

1758.

[Temporary.] [Royal Arms.] | Acts and Laws, | Passed by the Great and General Court or Assembly of His Ma- | jesty's Province of the Massachusetts-Bay in New-England: | Begun and Held at Boston, upon Wednesday the twenty-fifth | Day of May 1757. And continued by Prorogations and Ad- | journment to Tuesday the eighteenth Day of April following, | and then met. |

Colophon: Boston, N. E. | Printed by Samuel Kneeland, by Order of His Excellency | the Governour, Council, and House of Representa- | tives. 1758.

Collation: No title; pp. 349–354. B. H. L. P. S. W.

In some copies, pp. 350, 351, 353, 354, are misnumbered 450, 451, 453, 454.

1758.

[Temporary.] [Royal Arms.] | Acts and Laws, | Passed by the Great and General Court or Assembly of His Ma- | jesty's Province of the Massachusetts-Bay in New-England: | Begun and Held at Boston, upon Wednesday the thirty-first | Day of May 1758.

Colophon: Boston: N. E. | Printed by S. Kneeland, by Order of His Excellency the | Governour, Council, and House of Representa- | tives. 1758.

Collation: No title; pp. 355–363 [1]. B. H. L. P. S. W.

1758.

[Royal Arms.] | An Act | Passed by the Great and General Court or Assembly of the Province of the | Massachusetts-Bay in New-England; Begun and Held at Boston, on Wed- | nesday the Thirty-first Day of May 1758.

Colophon: Boston; in New-England: | Printed by John Draper, Printer to His Excellency the Governor | and Honorable His Majesty's Council, M, DCC, LVIII.

Collation: No title; pp. (7). S.

An Act for apportioning and assessing the Sum of Eighty-two Thousand and thirteen Pounds six Shillings and eight Pence.

1758.

[Royal Arms.] | An Act | Passed by the Great and General Court or Assembly of His Ma- | jesty's Province of the Massachusetts-Bay in New-England: | Begun and Held at Boston, upon Wednesday the thirty-first Day of May, 1758. And continued by sundry Prorogations | to the fourth Day of October following, and then met.

Colophon: Boston: Printed by S. Kneeland, by Order of his Excellency the | Governour, Council and House of Representatives. 1758.

Collation: No title; p. 495 [1]. H. L. P. S.

1758.

[Temporary.] [Royal Arms.] | Acts and Laws, | Passed by the Great and General Court or Assembly of His Ma- | jesty's Province of the Massachusetts-Bay in New-England: | Begun and Held at Boston, upon Wednesday the thirty-first | Day of May 1758. And continued by sundry Prorogations | to the fourth Day of October following, and then met.

Colophon: Boston: Printed by S. Kneeland, by Order of His | Excellency the Governour, Council and House of Re- | presentatives. 1758.

Collation: No title; pp. 365, 366. B. H. L. P. S. W.

1759.

[Royal Arms] | Acts and Laws, | Passed by the Great and General Court or Assembly of His Ma- | jesty's Province of the Massachusetts-Bay in New England: | Begun and Held at Boston, upon Wednesday the thirty-first | Day of May 1758. And continued by sundry Prorogations to | Friday the twenty-ninth Day of December following, and then | met.

Colophon: Boston; N. E. Printed by S. Kneeland, by Order | of His Excellency the Governour, Council and House of | Representatives. 1759.

Collation: No title; pp. 497–503 [1]. B. L. P. S.

The Boston Public Library copy has p. 503 torn.

1759.

[Temporary.] [Royal Arms.] | Acts and Laws, | Passed by the Great and General Court or Assembly of His Ma- | jesty's Province of the Massachusetts-Bay in New-England: | Begun and Held at Boston, upon Wednesday the thirty-first | Day of May 1758. And continued by sundry Prorogations to | Friday the twenty-ninth Day of December following, and then | met.

Colophon: Boston: N. E. Printed by S. Kneeland, by Order | of His Excellency the Governour, Council and House of | Representatives. 1759.

Collation: No title; pp. 367–372. B. H. L. P. S. W.

1759.

[Royal Arms.] | An Act, | Passed by the Great and General Court or Assembly of His Ma- | jesty's Province of the Massachusetts-Bay in New-England: | Begun and Held at Boston, upon Wednesday the thirty-first | Day of May 1758. And continued by sundry Prorogations to | Wednesday the twenty-eighth Day of February following, and | then met.

Colophon: Boston: N. E. | Printed by S. Kneeland, by Order of His Excellency the | Governour, Council, and House of Repre- | sentatives. 1759.

Collation: No title; pp. 505–508. L. P. S.

1759.

[Temporary.] [Royal Arms.] | Acts and Laws, | Passed by the Great and General Court or Assembly of His Ma- | jesty's Province of the Massachusetts-Bay in New-England: | Begun and Held at Boston, upon Wednesday the thirty-first | Day of May 1758. And continued by sundry Prorogations to | Wednesday the twenty-eighth Day of February following, and | then met.

Colophon: Boston: N. E. | Printed by S. Kneeland, by Order of His Excellency | the Governour, Council, and House of Repre-| sentatives. 1759.

Collation: No title; pp. 373–394. B. H. L. P. S. W.

1759.

[Temporary.] [Royal Arms.] | An Act, | Passed by the Great and General Court or Assembly of His Ma- | jesty's Province of the Massachusetts-Bay in New-England: | Begun and Held at Boston, upon Wednesday the thirty-first | Day of May 1758. And continued by sundry Prorogations | and Adjournment to Wednesday the eleventh Day of April | following, and then met.

Colophon: Boston: N. E. | Printed by Order of His Excellency the Governour, Council | and House of Representatives. And Sold by by [sic] S. Kneeland | in Queen-Street. M,DCC,LIX.

Collation: pp. 395–406. B. H. L. P. S. W.

1759.

[Royal Arms.] | An Act | Passed by the Great and General Court or Assembly of the Province of the | Massachusetts-Bay in New-England: Begun and Held at Boston, on Wed- | nesday the Thirtieth Day of May 1759.

Colophon: Boston in New-England: | Printed by John Draper, Printer to His Excellency the Governor, | and the Honorable His Majesty's Council, | 1759.

Collation: No title; pp. 7 [11]. S.

An Act for apportioning and assessing the Sum of Ninety-four Thousand seven Hundred and eighty Pounds three Shillings and two Pence.

1759.

[Royal Arms.] | Acts and Laws, | Passed by the Great and General Court or Assembly of His Ma- | jesty's Province of the Massachusetts-Bay in New-England: | Begun and Held at Boston, upon Wednesday the thirtieth | Day of May 1759.

Colophon: Boston: N. E. | Printed by S. Kneeland, by Order of His Excellency the | Governour, Council and House of Representatives. 1759.

Collation: No title: pp. 509, 510. L. P. S.

The Harvard College Library copy has N.B. for N.E. in the Colophon. The Lenox Library copy is mutilated.

1759.

[Temporary.] [Royal Arms.] | An Act | Passed by the Great and General Court or Assembly of His Ma- | jesty's Province of the Massachusetts-Bay in New-England: | Begun and held at Boston, upon Wednesday the thirtieth Day | of May, 1759.

Colophon: Boston: N. E. | Printed by S. Kneeland, by Order of His Excellency the Governour, | Council and House of Representatives. M,DCC,LIX.

Collation: No title; p. 407 [1]. B. H. L. P. S. W.

1759.

[Royal Arms.] | Acts and Laws, | Passed by the Great and General Court or Assembly of His Ma- | jesty's Province of the Massachusetts-Bay in New-England: | Begun and held at Boston, upon Wednesday the thirtieth Day | of May, 1759. And from thence continued by sundry Pro- | rogations to Wednesday the third Day of October following, | and then met.

Colophon: Boston: N. E. | Printed by S. Kneeland, by Order of His Excellency the Gover- | nour, Council and House of Representatives. M,DCC,LIX.

Collation: No title; pp. 511–514. L. P. S.

"In most copies the last page is misnumbered 420, and the error is carried on to the end of the volume. It was, however, detected in time to correct it in a few copies." (Hildeburn.) The Lenox Library copy is mutilated.

1759.

[Temporary.] [Royal Arms.] | Acts and Laws, | Passed by the Great and General Court or Assembly of His Ma- | jesty's Province of the Massachusetts-Bay in New-England: | Begun and held at Boston, upon Wednesday the thirtieth Day | of May 1759. And from thence continued by sundry Pro- | rogations to Wednesday the third Day of October following, | and then met.

Colophon: Boston: N. E. | Printed by S. Kneeland, by Order of His Excellency the Gover- | nour, Council and House of Representatives. M,DCC,LIX.

Collation: No title; pp. 409–420. B. H. L. P. S. W.

1759.

Acts | and | Laws, | Of His Majesty's | Province | of the | Massachusetts-Bay | in | New-England. | [Royal Arms.]

Boston, in New-England: | Printed by S. Kneeland, by Order of His Excellency the | Governor, Council and House of Representatives. | M,D,CC,LIX.

Collation: Title to Charter, 1 leaf; Charter, pp. 1–12; Explanatory charter, pp. 13, 14; Table, pp. 1–24; Title to Acts, 1 p.; Authorization, 1 p.; Acts, pp. 1–396. A. B. C. H. L. N. P. S. W.

A copy in the Boston Public Library belonged to Benjamin Franklin. In some copies, pp. 321–324 are misnumbered 319–322, there being no pages numbered 323, 324. Title to Charter reads:

The | Charter | Granted by their Majesties | King William | and | Queen Mary, | to the | Inhabitants | of the | Province | of the | Massachusetts-Bay | in | New-England. | Boston, in New-England: | Printed by S. Kneeland, by Order of His Excellency the | Governor, Council and House of Representatives. | M,DCC,LIX.[1]

1760.

[Royal Arms.] | Acts and Laws, | Passed by the Great and General Court or Assembly of His Ma- |jesty's Province of the Massachusetts-Bay in New-England: | Begun and held at Boston, upon Wednesday the thirteenth Day | of May, 1759. And from thence continued by sundry Pro- | rogations to Wednesday the second Day of January following, | and then met.

Colophon: Boston: N. E. | Printed by S. Kneeland, by Order of His Excellency the Gover- | nour, Council and House of Representatives. M,DCC,LX.

Collation: No title; pp. 421 [515]–424 [518]. L. P. S.

The Lenox Library copy has pp. 515, 516, mutilated.

1760.

[Temporary.] [Royal Arms.] | Acts and Laws, | Passed by the Great and General Court or Assembly of His Ma- | jesty's Province of the Massachusetts-Bay in New-England: | Begun and held at Boston, upon Wednesday the thirtieth Day | of May, 1759. And from thence continued by sundry Pro- | rogations to Wednesday the second Day of January following, | and then met.

Collation: No title; pp. 421–448. B. H. L. P. S. W.

1760.

An Act, | Passed by the Great and General Court or Assembly of His Ma- | jesty's Province of the Massachusetts-

[1] This volume, when complete, extends to p. 679.

Bay in New-England: | Begun and held at Boston upon Wednesday the thirtieth Day | of May, 1759. And from thence continued by sundry Proro- | gations to Wednesday the nineteenth of March following, and | then met.

Collation: No title; pp. 425 [519] [1]. P. S.

1760.

[Temporary.] [Royal Arms.] | Acts and Laws, | Passed by the Great and General Court or Assembly of His Ma- | jesty's Province of the Massachusetts-Bay in New-England: | Begun and held at Boston upon Wednesday the thirtieth Day | of May, 1759. And from thence continued by sundry Proro- | gations to Wednesday the nineteenth Day of March following, and | then met.

Colophon: Boston: N. E. | Printed by S. Kneeland, by Order of His Excellency the Gover- | nour, Council and House of Representatives. MDCCLX.

Collation: No title; pp. 449–455 [1]. B. H. L. P. S. W.

1760.

[Temporary.] [Royal Arms.] | Acts and Laws, | Passed by the Great and General Court or Assembly of His Ma- | jesty's Province of the Massachusetts-Bay in New-England: | Begun and held at Boston upon Wednesday the thirtieth Day | of May 1759. And from thence continued by sundry Proro- | gations and Adjournment to Wednesday the sixteenth of April | following, and then met.

Colophon: Boston: N. E. | Printed by S. Kneeland, by Order of His Excellency the Gover- | nor, Council and House of Representatives. MDCCLX.

Collation: No title; pp. 457–466. B. H. L. P. S. W.

1760.

[Royal Arms.] | Acts and Laws, | Passed by the Great and General Court or Assembly of His Ma- | jesty's Province of the Massachusetts-Bay in New-England: | Begun and held at Boston, upon Wednesday the twenty-eighth | Day of May, 1760.

Colophon: Boston: N. E. | Printed by S. Kneeland, by Order of His Honour the Lieutenant | Governor, Council and House of Representatives. | M.DCC.LX

Collation: No title; pp. 427 [521]–432 [526]. L. P. S.

The Lenox Library copy lacks pp. 523–526.

1760.

[Temporary.] [Royal Arms.] | Acts and Laws, | Passed by the Great and General Court or Assembly of His Ma- | jesty's Province of the Massachusetts-Bay in New-England: | Begun and held at Boston, upon Wednesday the twenty-eighth | Day of May 1760.

Colophon: Boston: N. E. | Printed by S. Kneeland, by Order of His Honour the Lieutenant | Governour, Council and House of Representatives: | M,DCC,LX.

Collation: No title; pp. 467–477 [1]. B. H. L. P. S. W.

1760.

[Royal Arms.] | An Act | Passed by the Great and General Court or Assembly of the Province of the | Massachusetts-Bay in New-England: Begun and Held at Boston, on Wednes- | day the Twenty-eighth Day of May 1760.

Colophon: Boston; New-England: | Printed by John Draper, Printed to His Honour the Lieutenant-Governour, and | the Honorable His Majesty's Council. | 1760.

Collation: No title; pp. 7 [11]. L. P. S.

An Act for apportioning and assessing the Sum of Ninety-four Thousand eight Hundred and seventy-seven Pounds eleven Shillings.

1760.

[Temporary.] [Royal Arms.] | Acts and Laws, | Passed by the Great and General Court or Assembly of his Ma- | jesty's Province of the Massachusetts-Bay in New-England: | Begun and held at Boston, upon Wednesday the twenty-eighth | Day of May, 1760. And from thence continued by Proro- | gation to Wednesday the thirteenth Day of August following, | and then met.

Colophon: Boston: N. E. | Printed by Order of His Excellency the Governour, Council and | House of Representatives. M,DCC,LX.

Collation: No title; pp. 479, 480. H. L. P. S. W.

1761.

[Temporary.] [Royal Arms.] | Acts and Laws, | Passed by the Great and General Court or Assembly of His Ma- | jesty's Province of the Massachusetts-Bay in New-England: | Begun and held at Boston, upon Wednesday the twenty-eighth | Day of May, 1760. And from thence continued by Proro- | gations to Wednesday the seventeenth Day of December | following, and then met.

Colophon: Boston: N. E. | Printed by S. Kneeland, by Order of the Governor, | Council and House of Representatives, MDCCLXI.

Collation: No title; pp. 481–491 [1]. H. L. P. S. W.

The Pennsylvania Historical Society's copy is imperfect. The Lenox Library copy lacks pp. 481–484.

1761.

An Act, | Passed by the Great and General Court or Assembly of his Majesty's | Province of the Massachusetts-Bay in New England: Begun and | held at Boston, upon Wednesday the twenty-eighth Day of | May, 1760. And from thence continued by Prorogations to | Wednesday the seventeenth Day of December following, and | then met.

Colophon: Boston: N. E. | Printed by S. Kneeland, by Order of his Excellency the Governor, | Council and House of Representatives. 1761.

Collation: No title; pp. 1–4. L.

An Act for Repealing the several Laws now in Force which relate to the Observation of the Lord's-Day.

1761.

[Temporary.] [Royal Arms.] | An Act, | Passed by the Great and General Court or Assembly of his Ma- | jesty's Province of the Massachusetts-Bay in New-England: | Begun and held at Boston, upon Wednesday the twenty-eighth | Day of May, 1760. And from thence continued by Proro- | gations to Wednesday the twenty-fifth Day of March fol- | lowing, and then met.

Colophon: Boston: N. E. | Printed by S. Kneeland, by Order of the Governor, | Council and House of Representatives. 1761.

Collation: No title; pp. 493–498. H. S. W.

1761.

[Temporary.] [Royal Arms.] | An Act, | Passed by the Great and General Court or Assembly of his Ma- | jesty's Province of the Massachusetts-Bay in New-England: | Begun and held at Boston, upon Wednesday the twenty-eighth | Day of May, 1760. And from thence continued by Proro- | gations to Wednesday the twenty-fifth Day of March fol- | lowing, and then met.

Collation: No title; pp. 493, 494. L.

1761.

[Royal Arms.] | An Act, | Passed by the Great and General Court or Assembly of His Majesty's | Province of the

Massachusetts-Bay in New-England: Begun and | held at Boston, upon Wednesday the twenty-eighth Day of May, | 1760. And continued by Prorogations until Wednesday the | twenty-fifth of March following, and then met.

Colophon: Boston: N. E. | Printed by S. Kneeland, by Order of his Excellency the Governor, | Council and House of Representatives. 1761.

Collation: No title; pp. 397–403 [1].

A. B. C. H. L. N. P. S. W.

1761.

[Royal Arms.] | Acts and Laws, | Passed by the Great and General Court or Assembly of His Majesty's | Province of the Massachusetts-Bay in New-England: Begun and | held at Boston, upon Wednesday the twenty-seventh Day of May, | 1761.

Colophon: Boston: N. E. | Printed by S. Kneeland, by Order of his Excellency the Governor, | Council and House of Representatives. 1761.

Collation: No title; pp. 405–409 [1].

A. B. C. H. L. N. P. S. W.

1761.

[Royal Arms.] | An Act | Passed by the Great and General Court or Assembly of the Province of the | Massachusetts-Bay in New-England: Begun and Held at Boston, on Wednes- | day the Twenty-seventh Day of May 1761.

Colophon: Boston; New-England: | Printed by John Draper, Printer to His Excellency the Governor, | and the Honorable His Majesty's Council. | 1761.

Collation: No title; pp. 7 [11]. S.

An Act for apportioning and assessing the Sum of Seventy-five Thousand Pounds.

1761.

[Temporary.] [Royal Arms.] | Acts and Laws, | Passed by the Great and General Court or Assembly of His Ma-| jesty's Province of the Massachusetts-Bay in New-England: | Begun and held at Boston, upon Wednesday the twenty- | seventh Day of May 1761.

Colophon: Boston: N. E. | Printed by S. Kneeland, by Order of the Governor, | Council and House of Representatives. 1761.

Collation: No title; pp. 499–509 [1]. B. H. L. P. S. W.

1761.

[Royal Arms.] | Acts and Laws, | Passed by the Great and General Court or Assembly of his Ma- | jesty's Province of the Massachusetts-Bay in New-England: | Begun and held at Boston, upon Wednesday the twenty-sixth | Day of May, 1756. And continued by sundry Prorogations | to the sixth Day of January following, and then met.

Collation: No title; pp. 411–414. A. B. C. H. L. N. P. S. W.

In the margin of p. 411 is the following: "*Note*, The three following Acts were omitted in their proper place, *Page* 375."

1761.

[Royal Arms.] | Acts and Laws, | Passed by the Great and General Court or Assembly of His Ma- | jesty's Province of the Massachusetts-Bay in New-England, | Begun and held at Boston, upon Wednesday the twenty-seventh | Day of May, 1761. and continued by sundry Prorogations | unto Thursday the twelfth Day of November following and | then met.

Colophon: Boston: N. E. | Printed by S. Kneeland, by Order of his Excellency the | Governor, Council and House of Representatives. | M,DCC,LXI.

Collation: No title; pp. 415–418. A. B. C. H. L. P. S. W.

1761.

[Royal Arms.] Acts and Laws, | Passed by the Great and General Court or Assembly of his Ma- | jesty's Province of the Massachusetts Bay in New-England, | Begun and held at Boston, upon Wednesday the twenty-seventh | Day of May, 1761. and continued by sundry Prorogations | unto Wednesday the thirteenth Day of January following, | and then met.

Colophon: Boston, N. E. | Printed by S. Kneeland, by Order of his Excellency the | Governor, Council and House of Representatives. | M,DCC,LXII.

Collation: No title; pp. 419–429 [1]. A. B. C. H. L. P. S. W.

1762.

[Temporary.] [Royal Arms.] | Acts and Laws, | Passed by the Great and General Court or Assembly of his Ma- | jesty's Province of the Massachusetts-Bay in New-England, | Begun and held at Boston, upon Wednesday the twenty-seventh | Day of May, 1761. and continued by sundry Prorogations | unto Wednesday the thirteenth Day of January following, | and then met.

Colophon: Boston: Printed by S. Kneeland, by Order of his | Excellency the Governor, Council and House of | Representatives. M,DCC,LXII.

Collation: No title; pp. 511–536. B. H. L. P. S. W.

1762.

[Royal Arms.] | Acts and Laws, | Passed by the Great and General Court or Assembly of his Ma- | jesty's Province of the Massachusetts-Bay in New-England, | Begun and held at Boston, upon Wednesday the twenty-seventh | Day of May, 1761. and continued by sundry Prorogations | unto

Wednesday the fourteenth Day of April following and | then met.

Colophon: Boston: N. E. | Printed by S. Kneeland, by Order of his Excellency the | Governor, Council and House of Representatives. | M,DCC,LXII.

Collation: No title; pp. 430 [431], 431 [432].
A. B. C. H. L. P. S. W.

1762.

[Temporary.] [Royal Arms.] | Acts and Laws, | Passed by the Great and General Court or Assembly of his Ma- | jesty's Province of the Massachusetts-Bay in New-England, Be- | gun and held at Boston, upon Wednesday the twenty-seventh | Day of May, 1761. and continued by sundry Prorogations | unto Wednesday the fourteenth Day of April following and | then met.

Colophon: Boston: Printed by S. Kneeland, by Order of His Excel- | lency the Governor Council & House of Representatives. | M,DCC,LXII.

Collation: No title; pp. 537–540. B. L. P. S. W.

1762.

[Royal Arms.] | Acts and Laws, | Passed by the Great and General Court or Assembly of his Ma- | jesty's Province of the Massachusetts-Bay in New-England: | Begun and held at Boston, upon Wednesday the twenty-sixth | Day of May, 1762.

Colophon: Boston, N. E. | Printed by S. Kneeland, by Order of his Excellency the | Governor, Council and House of Representatives. | M,DCC,LXII.

Collation: No title; pp. 433–436. A. B. C. H. L. P. S. W.

1762.

[Temporary.] [Royal Arms.] | Acts and Laws, | Passed by the Great and General Court or Assembly of his | Majesty's Province of the Massachusetts-Bay, in New-En- | gland: Begun and held at Boston, upon Wednesday the | twenty-sixth Day of May, 1762.

Collation: No title; pp. 541–550. B. L. P. W.

The American Antiquarian Society's copy lacks pp. 549, 550.

1762.

[Royal Arms.] | An Act | Passed by the Great and General Court or Assembly of the Province of the Massachusetts- | Bay in New-England: Begun and held at Boston, on Wednesday the Twenty-sixth | Day of May 1762.

Colophon: Boston; New-England: | Printed by John Draper, Printer to His Excellency the Governour, and | the Honorable His Majesty's Council. | 1762.

Collation: No title; pp. 7 [11]. P. S.

An Act for apportioning and assessing the Sum of Seventy-five Thousand Pounds.

1762.

[Royal Arms.] | Acts and Laws, | Passed by the Great and General Court or Assembly of his Ma- | jesty's Province of the Massachusetts-Bay in New-England: | Begun and held at Boston, upon Wednesday the twenty-sixth | Day of May, 1762. And continued by Prorogations to Wed- | nesday the eighth of September following, and then met.

Colophon: Boston, N. E. | Printed by S. Kneeland, by Order of His Excellency the | Governor, Council and House of Representatives. | M,DCC,LXII.

Collation: No title; pp. 437–439 [1]. B. C. H. L. P. S. W.

1763.

[Royal Arms.] Acts and Laws, | Passed by the Great and General Court or Assembly of his Majesty's | Province of the Massachusetts-Bay in New-England: Begun and | held at Boston, upon Wednesday the twenty-sixth Day of May, | 1762. and continued by Prorogations to Wednesday the twelfth | of January following, and then met.

Colophon: Boston, N. E. Printed by S. Kneeland, by Order of his Excellency | the Governor, Council and House of Representatives. 1763.

Collation: No title; pp. 441–444. B. C. H. L. P. S. W.

1763.

Temporary Acts and Laws | Of His Majesty's | Province | of the | Massachusetts-Bay | in | New-England. | [Royal Arms.]

Boston; New-England: | Printed by Order of His Excellency the Governor, | Council and House of Representatives: | And Sold by Green and Russell in Queen-Street. | MDCCLXIII.

Collation: title, 1 p.; Authorization, 1 p.; Table, pp. i–x; Note, 1 leaf; Titles (to p. 179), pp. i–viii; Laws, pp. 1–179 [1].[1] A. B. C. H. L. P. S. W.

1763.

[Temporary.] The Acts | Contained in this Book were | ordered to be left out of the | last Impression of Tempo- | rary Laws and printed by | themselves, viz. | Impost Act, from Page 1 to 8 | Act for granting an Excise upon Spirits, &c. | 9 to 22 | Act for providing and maintaining two armed | Vessels, &c. 23 to 29 | Acts respecting the Poor, 29 to 38 | Acts respecting High-Ways, 39 to 43 | Acts respecting Alewives and other Fish, 43 to 51 | Acts respecting Deer, 52 | [Royal Arms.]

Boston; New-England. | Printed by Green and Russell, by Order of his Excel- | lency the Governor, Council and House of | Representatives. MDCCLXIII.

Collation: Title, 1 leaf; Acts, pp. 1–52. B. L. P. S W.

---

[1] This volume, when complete, extends to p. 528.

1763.

[Royal Arms.] | Acts and Laws, | Passed by the Great and General Court or Assembly of his | Majesty's Province of the Massachusetts-Bay in New-England: | Begun and held at Boston, upon Wednesday the twenty- | fifth Day of May, 1763.

Colophon: Boston: N. E. | Printed by S. Kneeland, by Order of His Excellency the | Governor, Council and House of Representatives. | M,DCC,LXIII.

Collation: No title; pp. 445–450. B. C. H. L. P. S. W.

1763.

[Royal Arms.] | An Act | Passed by the Great and General Court or Assembly of the Province of the Massachusetts- | Bay in New-England: Begun and held at Boston, on Wednesday the Twenty-fifth | Day of May, 1763.

Colophon: Boston: Printed by Richard Draper, Printer to His Excellency the | Governor and the Honorable His Majesty's Council. 1763.

Collation: No title; pp. 9 [13]. P. S.

An Act for apportioning and assessing a Tax of Fifty Thousand Pounds. The Massachusetts State Library copy lacks p. 9.

1763.

[Temporary.] [Royal Arms.] | Acts and Laws, | Passed by the Great and General Court or Assembly of | his Majesty's Province of the Massachusetts-Bay | in New-England: Begun and held at Boston, upon | Wednesday the twenty-fifth Day of May, 1763.

Colophon: Boston: N. E. | Printed by Green and Russell, by Order of His Excel- | lency the Governor, Council, and House of | Representatives. 1763.

Collation: No title; pp. 181–190. A. B. C. H. L. P. S. W.

1764.

[Royal Arms.] | Acts and Laws, | Passed by the Great and General Court or Assembly of his Ma- | jesty's Province of the Massachusetts-Bay in New-England: | Begun and held at Boston, upon Wednesday the twenty-fifth | Day of May 1763, and continued by Prorogations to Wed- | nesday the twenty-second Day of December next, and then met.

Colophon: Boston: N. E. | Printed by S. Kneeland, by Order of His Excellency the | Governor, Council and House of Representatives. | M,DCC,LXIV.

Collation: No title; pp. 451–455 [1]. B. C. H. L. P. S. W.

1764.

[Temporary.] [Royal Arms.] | Acts and Laws, | Passed by the Great and General Court or Assembly | of his Majesty's Province of the Massachusetts-Bay | in New-England: Begun and held at Boston, upon | Wednesday the twenty-fifth Day of May, 1763. | And continued by sundry Prorogations to Wednes- | day the twenty-first Day of December following, | and then met.

Colophon: Boston: Printed by Green and Russell, by Order of his | Excellency the Governor, Council, and House of | Representatives. 1764.

Collation: No title; pp. 191–202. B. H. L. P. S. W.

1764.

[Royal Arms.] | Acts and Laws, | Passed by the Great and General Court or Assembly of his Majesty's | Province of the Massachusetts-Bay in New-England: Begun | and held at Concord, upon Wednesday the thirtieth Day of | May, 1764.

Colophon: Boston: | Printed by S. Kneeland, by Order of His Excellency the Governor, | Council and House of Representatives. MDCCLXIV.

Collation: No title; pp. 157, 158. B. C. H. L. P. S. W.

1764.

[Temporary.] [Royal Arms.] | Acts and Laws, | Passed by the Great and General Court or Assembly of | his Majesty's Province of the Massachusetts-Bay in | New-England: Begun and held at Concord, upon | Wednesday the Thirtieth Day of May, 1764.

Colophon: Boston; N. E. Printed by Green and Russell, by Order of | His Excellency the Governor, Council and House of | Representatives. 1764.

Collation: No title; pp. 203–213 [1]. B. H. L. P. S. W.

1764.

[Royal Arms.] | An Act | Passed by the Great and General Court or Assembly of the Province of the Massachusetts-Bay in | New-England; begun and held at Concord, on Wednesday the Thirtieth Day of May, 1764.

Colophon: Boston: | Printed by Richard Draper, Printer to His Excellency the Governor, and | the Honorable His Majesty's council. 1764.

Collation: No title; pp. 8 [13]. P. S.

An Act for apportioning and assessing a Tax of Fifty Thousand Pounds.

1764.

[Royal Arms.] | An Act of Parliament, | Passed in the Sixth Year of the Reign of His Majesty | King George the Second. 1733.

Collation: No title; pp. 459–463. B. C. H. H^L^. L. P. S. W.

An Act for the better securing and encouraging the Trade of His Majesty's Sugar Colonies in America. In some copies pp. 460, 461, 462, are misnumbered 160, 161, 162, or 160, 161, 164. The pages of the Harvard Law School Library copy are numbered correctly. This item was issued with the next.

1764.

[Royal Arms.] | An Act of Parliament, passed in the | Fourth Year of the Reign of His Majesty King | George the Third. 1764.

Collation: No title; pp. 464–479. B. C. H. H^{L}. L. P. S. W.

An Act for granting certain Duties in the British Colonies and Plantations in America. In some copies, pp. 471 to 479 are misnumbered 469 to 477. One copy in the Boston Public Library is correctly paged, the other has pp. 470, 473, 474, misnumbered 670, 463, 674. The Harvard Law School Library copy is a different edition from the Harvard College Library copy. This item was issued with the preceding.

Two different editions of pp. 459–479 were issued. They differ in the captions on pp. 459, 464, in the Royal Arms on pp. 459, 464, and in the arrangement of lines; and in one edition the W in "Whereas," the first word of the Act beginning on p. 459, is a plain four-line letter, while in the other edition it is an ornamental initial letter.

1764.

Two | Acts of Parliament, | One passed in the Sixth Year of the Reign of | King George the Second: | For Encouraging the Trade of the British Sugar Colonies. | The other, passed in the Fourth Year of the Reign | of King George the Third: | For Granting certain Duties in the British Colonies. | [Royal Arms.]

London: Printed by the King's Printer. | Boston, N. E. Reprinted by Richard Draper, Prin- | ter to His Excellency the Governor and the Honorable | His Majesty's Council of the Province of Massachusetts | Bay. M.DCC.LXIV.

Collation: Title, 1 leaf; Text, pp. 459–477 [479] [1]. W.

1764.

[Royal Arms.] | Acts and Laws, | Passed by the Great and General Court or Assembly of His Ma- | jesty's Province of the Massachusetts-Bay, in New-England: | Begun and held at Concord, upon Wednesday the thirtieth Day | of May, 1764. And continued by sundry Prorogations to |

Thursday the eighteenth Day of October following, and then | met at Boston.

Colophon: Boston: Printed by S. Kneeland, by Order of His Excellency the | Governor, Council and House of Representatives. 1764.

Collation: No title; pp. 481, 482. B. C. H. L. P. S. W.

In some copies, these pages are numbered 479, 480. The Boston Public Library has a copy of each issue. Throughout the remainder of the volume there is an error of two pages.

1764.

[Temporary.] [Royal Arms.] | An Act, | Passed by the Great and General Court or Assembly | of his Majesty's Province of the Massachusetts-Bay | in New-England: Begun and held at Concord, in | the County of Middlesex, upon Wednesday the | Thirtieth Day of May, 1764; and from thence | continued by sundry Prorogations to Thursday the | Eighteenth Day of October following, and then | met at Boston, in the County of Suffolk.

Boston, N. E. Printed by Green & Russell, by Order of his Excellency | the Governor, Council, and House of Representatives, 1764.

Collation: No title; p. 215 [1]. B. H. L. P. S. W.

1764.

[Hutchinson, Thomas.] The Case | Of the Provinces of | Massachusetts-Bay | and | New-York, | Respecting the Boundary Line be- | tween the two Provinces. | [Royal Arms.]

Boston; New-England, | Printed by Green and Russell, by Order of His Excellency the | Governor, the Honorable his Majesty's Council, and | the Honorable House of Representatives. 1764.

Collation: Title, 1 p.; Text, pp. ii–xxx. H. M. S.

1765.

[Royal Arms.] | Acts and Laws, | Passed by the Great and General Court or Assembly | of His Majesty's Province of the Massachusetts-Bay | in New-England: Begun and held at Concord | in the County of Middlesex, upon Wednesday the | Thirtieth Day of May, 1764, and from thence | continued by sundry Prorogations to Wednesday the | Ninth Day of January following, and then met at | Boston in the County of Suffolk.

Colophon: Boston; New-England: | Printed by Richard and Samuel Draper, and Green and Russell, | Printers to the Government. 1765.

Collation: No title; pp. 481–489 [1]. B. C. H. L. P. S. W.

1765.

[Temporary.] [Royal Arms.] | Acts and Laws, | Passed by the Great and General Court or Assembly | of his Majesty's Province of the Massachusetts-Bay | in New-England: Begun and held at Concord, in | the County of Middlesex, upon Wednesday the | Thirtieth Day of May, 1764; and from thence | continued by sundry Prorogations to Wednesday | the Ninth Day of January following, and then | met at Boston, in the County of Suffolk. |

Colophon: Boston; New-England: | Printed by Richard and Samuel Draper, and Green and Russell, | Printers to the Government. 1765.

Collation: No title; pp. 217–263 [1]. B. H. L. P. S. W.

1765.

Anno Regni | Georgii III. | Regis | Magnæ Britanniæ, Franciæ, & Hiberniæ, | Quinto. | At the Parliament begun and holden at Westmin- | ster, the Nineteenth Day of May, Anno Dom. | 1761, in the First Year of the Reign of | our

Sovereign Lord George the Third, by | the Grace of God, of Great Britain, France, and | Ireland, King, Defender of the Faith, &c. | And from thence continued by several Prorogations to the Tenth | Day of January, 1765, being the Fourth Session of the Twelfth Parliament of Great Britain. | [Royal Arms.]

London. | Printed by Mark Baskett, Printer to the King's most Excel- | lent Majesty; and by the Assigns of Robert Baskett. 1765.

Collation: Title, 1 leaf; Text, pp. 279–310. B.

The Stamp Act.

1765.

Anno Regni | Georgii III. | Regis | Magnæ Britanniæ, Franciæ, & Hiberniæ, | Quinto. | At the Parliament begun and holden at | Westminster, the Nineteenth Day of | May, Anno Dom. 1761, in the First | Year of the Reign of our Sove- | reign Lord George the Third, | by the Grace of God, of Great Britain, | France, and Ireland, King, Defender | of the Faith, &c. | And from thence continued by several Prorogations to | the Tenth Day of January, 1765, being the Fourth | Session of the Twelfth Parliament of Great Britain. | [Royal Arms.]

London: | Printed by Mark Baskett, Printer to the King's most | Excellent Majesty; and by the Assigns of Robert | Baskett. M.DCC.LXV.

Collation: Title, 1 leaf; Text, pp. 3–66. Quarto. M.

The Stamp Act.

1765.

Anno Regni | Georgii III. | Regis | Magnæ Britanniæ, Franciæ & Hiberniæ, | Quinto. | At the Parliament begun and holden at Westminster, | the Nineteenth Day of May, Anno Dom. 1761, | in the First Year of the Reign of our Sovereign | Lord George the Third, by the Grace of God, | of Great Britain, France and Ireland, King, | Defender of the

Faith, &c. | And from thence continued by several Prorogations to the Tenth | Day of January, 1765, being the Fourth Session of the Twelfth | Parliament of Great Britain. | [Royal Arms.]

London Printed: | Boston, N. E. | Re-printed and Sold by Edes & Gill, in Queen- | Street. 1765.

Collation: Title, 1 leaf; Text, pp. 3–24. M. W.

The Stamp Act.

1765.

[Royal Arms.] | Acts and Laws, | Passed by the Great and General Court or Assembly | of His Majesty's Province of Massachusetts-Bay in | New-England: Begun and held at Boston, in the | County of Suffolk, upon Wednesday the Twenty- | ninth Day of May, 1765.

Colophon: Boston: Printed by Richard and Samuel Draper, and | Green and Russell, Printers to the Government. 1765.

Collation: No title; pp. 491–497 [1]. B. C. H. L. P. S. W.

1765.

[Temporary.] [Royal Arms.] | Acts and Laws, | Passed by the Great and General Court or Assembly | of his Majesty's Province of the Massachusetts-Bay | in New-England: Begun and held at Boston, upon | Wednesday the twenty-ninth Day of May, 1765.

Colophon: Boston; New-England: | Printed by Richard and Samuel Draper, and Green and Russell, | Printers to the Government. 1765.

Collation: No title; pp. 265–280. B. H. L. P. S. W.

1765.

[Royal Arms.] | An Act | Passed by the Great and General Court or Assembly of the Province of the Massachu-

1766.

[Royal Arms.] | Acts and Laws, | Passed by the Great and General Court or Assembly | of His Majesty's Province of Massachusetts-Bay in | New-England: Begun and held at Boston, in the | County of Suffolk, upon Wednesday the Twenty- | eighth Day of May, 1766.

Collation: No title; p. 505 [1]. B. C. H. L. P. S. W.

1766.

[Temporary.] [Royal Arms.] | Acts and Laws, | Passed by the Great and General Court or Assembly | of His Majesty's Province of the Massachusetts-Bay | in New-England: Begun and held at Boston in | the County of Suffolk upon Wednesday the Twen- | ty-eighth Day of May, 1766.

Colophon: Boston, New England: | Printed by Richard and Samuel Draper, & Green | and Russell, Printers to the Government. 1766.

Collation: No title; pp. 317–323 [1]. B. H. L. P. S. W.

1766.

[Royal Arms.] | An Act | Passed by the Great and General Court or Assembly of the Province of the Massachusetts-Bay, in | New-England; begun and held at Boston in the County of Suffolk on Wednesday the Twenty- | eighth Day of May, 1766.

Colophon: Boston: Printed by Richard and Samuel Draper and | Green and Russell, Printers to the Government. 1766.

Collation: No title; pp. 8 [13]. L. P. S.

An Act for apportioning and assessing a Tax of Forty Thousand Pounds.

1766.

The following Bill now pending in the House of Represen- | tatives, is published by their Order, for the Consideration of | the several Towns in this Province. | A Bill intituled, An Act for granting Compensation to the | Sufferers, and of free and general Pardon, Indemnity and | Oblivion to the Offenders in the late Times.

Colophon: Boston: Printed by Green and Russell, Printers to the | Honorable House of Representatives. 1766.

Collation: No title; pp. 1–4. B. L. W.

A Bill to grant compensation to Thomas Hutchinson, Andrew Oliver, Benjamin Hallowell, and William Story. Besides the Bill, there is a letter from Henry S. Conway to Governor Bernard, and two letters by Dennys De Berdt dated August 11 and September 19, 1766.

1766.

[Royal Arms.] | An Act of Parliament | Passed in the Sixth Year of the Reign of His Majesty | King George the Third. 1766.

Colophon: Boston: | Printed by Richard and Samuel Draper, and Green and Russell, | Printers to the Government. 1766.

Collation: No title; pp. 507–518. B. C. H. P. S. W.

The Act repealing the Stamp Act (pp. 507-517) and the "Indemnifying Act" (pp. 517, 518).

1766.

[Temporary.] [Royal Arms.] | An Act of Parliament, | Passed in the Sixth Year of the Reign of Our | Sovereign Lord George the Third.

Collation: No title; pp. 325–333 [1]. B. H. L. P. S. W.

An Act for opening, etc., certain Ports in Jamaica and Dominica.

1766.

[Temporary.] [Royal Arms.] | An Act of Parliament, | Passed in the Sixth Year of the Reign of Our | Sovereign Lord George the Third.

Collation: No title; pp. 335–347 [1]. B. H. L. P. S. W.

An Act to amend and render more effectual in His Majesty's Dominions in America, An Act for punishing Mutiny and Desertion.

1766.

[Royal Arms.] | Acts and Laws, | Passed by the Great and General Court or Assembly of His | Majesty's Province of the Massachusetts-Bay, in New-Eng- | land: Begun and held at Boston, upon Wednesday the | twenty-eighth Day of May, 1766; and from thence con- | tinued by several Prorogations to Wednesday the twenty- | ninth of October following, and then met.

Colophon: Boston: | Printed by Richard and Samuel Draper, and Green and Russell, | Printers to the Government. 1766.

Collation: No title; pp. 519–521 [1]. B. C. H. L. P. S. W.

1767.

Acts and Laws, | Passed by the Great and General Court or Assembly of | His Majesty's Province of the Massachusetts-Bay, in | New-England: January 1766 [1767].

Colophon: Boston: | Printed by Richard Draper, and Green and Russell, | Printers to the Government. 1767.

Collation: No title; pp. 523–530. B. C. H. L. P. S. W.

In some copies p 529 is misnumbered 526.

1767.

[Temporary.] [Royal Arms.] | Acts and Laws, | Passed by the Great and General Court or Assembly of | His Majesty's Province of the Massachusetts-Bay, in | New-England: Begun and held at Boston, upon | Wednesday the twenty-eighth Day of May 1766; | and from thence continued by several Prorogations | to Wednesday the twenty-ninth Day of January | following and then met.

Colophon: Boston, New-England: | Printed by Richard Draper, and Green and Russell, | Printers to the Government. 1767.

Collation: No title; pp. 349–364. B. H. L. P. S. W.

1767.

[Royal Arms.] | Acts and Laws, | Passed by the Great and General Court or Assembly | of His Majesty's Province of the Massachusetts-Bay | in New England: Begun and held at Boston, in | the County of Suffolk, upon Wednesday the Twen- | ty-seventh of May, 1767.

Colophon: Boston, New England. | Printed by Richard Draper, John Green, and Joseph | Russell, Printers to the Government. 1767.

Collation: No title; pp. 531–534. B. C. H. L. P. S. W.

"In the regular issue this sheet is Xxxx, but some copies were issued Vvvv" (Hildeburn). Both varieties are in the Pennsylvania Historical Society and the Lenox Library.

1767.

[Temporary.] [Royal Arms.] | Acts and Laws, | Passed by the Great and General Court or Assembly | of His Majesty's Province of the Massachusetts-Bay | in New-England: Begun and held at Boston, in | the County of Suffolk upon Wednesday the Twen- | ty-seventh Day of May 1767.

Colophon: Boston, New-England. | Printed by Richard Draper, John Green, and Joseph | Russell, Printers to the Government. 1767.

Collation: No title; pp. 365–371 [1]. B. H. L. P. S. W.

1767.

[Royal Arms.] | An Act | Passed by the Great and General Court or Assembly of the Province of Massachusetts-Bay, in | New-England; begun and held at Boston in the County of Suffolk, on Wednesday the | Twenty-seventh Day of May, 1767.

Colophon: Boston: Printed by Richard Draper and Green & Russell, | Printers to the Government. 1767.

Collation: No title; pp. 10 [14]. H. L. S.

An Act for apportioning and assessing a Tax of Forty Thousand Pounds.

1767.

[Royal Arms.] | An Act of Parliament, | Passed in the Seventh Year of the Reign of Our | Sovereign Lord George the Third.

Collation: No title; pp. 535–542. B. C. H. L. P. S. W.

An Act for granting certain Duties in the British Colonies and Plantations in America.

1768.

[Royal Arms.] | Acts and Laws, |Passed by the Great and General Court or Assembly | of the Province of Massachusetts-Bay, in New- | England, begun and held at Boston, the Twenty- | seventh Day of May 1767, and continued by se- | veral Prorogations to Wednesday the 30th of De- | cember following, and then met.

Colophon: Boston; New England, | Printed by Richard Draper, and Green & Russell, Printers | to the Government, 1768.

Collation: No title; pp. 543–548. B. C. H. L. P. S. W.

1768.

[Temporary.] [Royal Arms.] | Acts and Laws, | Passed by the Great and General Court or Assembly, of the | Province of Massachusetts-Bay, in New-England, begun | and held at Boston, the Twenty-seventh Day of May, | 1767, and continued by several Prorogations to Wednes- | day the 30th of December following, and then met.

Colophon: Boston: New-England, | Printed by Richard Draper, and Green & Russell, Printers | to the Government, 1768.

Collation: No title; pp. 373–388. B. H. L. P. S. W.

Colophon is printed on p. 380 as well as on p. 388.

1768.

[Royal Arms.] | Acts and Laws, | Passed by the Great and General Court or Assembly | of the Province of Massachusetts-Bay, in New- | England, begun and held at Boston, the Twenty- | fifth Day of May, 1768.

Colophon: Boston; N. E. | Printed by Richard Draper, and Green and Russell, Printers | to the Government. 1768.

Collation: No title; pp. 549–560. B. H. L. P. S. W.

Pages 559, 560, contain an Act of Parliament passed in 1767 to amend an Act for repealing certain Duties in the British Colonies and Plantations.

1768.

[Temporary.] [Royal Arms.] | Acts and Laws, | Passed by the Great and General Court or Assembly | of his Majesty's Province of the Massachusetts-Bay | in New-England: Begun and held at Boston, in | the County of Suffolk upon Wednesday the Twen- | ty-fifth Day of May 1768.

Collation: No title; pp. 389–402. B. H. L. P. S. W.

On p. 402 is printed an Act of Parliament for further continuing an Act to amend and render more effectual an Act for punishing Mutiny and Desertion.

1769.

[Royal Arms.] | An Act | Passed by the Great and General Court or Assembly of the Province of the | Massachusetts-Bay in New-England; begun and held at Boston, in the County | of Suffolk, on Wednesday the Thirty-first Day of May, 1769.

Colophon: Boston: Printed by Richard Draper, and Green and Russell, | Printers to the Government. 1769.

Collation: No title; pp. 8 [13]. P.

An Act for apportioning and assessing a Tax of Thirty Thousand Pounds.

1769.

[Temporary.] [Royal Arms.] | Acts and Laws, | Passed by the Great and General Court or Assembly | of His Majesty's Province of the Massachusetts- | Bay, in New-

England: Begun and held at Boston, | upon Wednesday the Thirty-first Day of May, 1769.

Colophon: Boston, New-England: | Printed by Richard Draper, and Green & Russell, | Printers to the Government. 1769.

Collation: No title; pp. 403–415 [1]. B. H. L. P. S. W.

1769.

The following is the Apportion of £92500, laid upon the several Towns, | Districts and Parishes, by Harrison Gray, Esq; Treasurer and Receiver-General, | by Virtue of an Act of the Great and General Court, made and passed at | their Session in June 1769.

Collation: No title; pp. 4. S.

1770.

[Temporary.] [Royal Arms.] |Acts and Laws, | Passed by the Great and General Court or Assembly | of His Majesty's Province of the Massachusetts- | Bay, in New-England: Begun and held at Boston, | upon Wednesday the thirty-first Day of May, | 1769; from thence continued by sundry Proro- | gations to Wednesday the Fifteenth Day of | March following, and then met at Cambridge in | the County of Middlesex.

Colophon: Boston, N. E. Printed by Richard Draper, and Green and | Russell, Printers to the Government. 1770.

Collation: No title; pp. 417–428. B. H. L. P. S. W.

1770.

[Royal Arms.] | Acts and Laws, | Passed by the Great and General Court or Assembly of the | Province of the Massachusetts-Bay in New-England, begun | and held at Boston, the Thirty-first Day of May, 1770; and | continued by sundry Prorogations to Thursday the Fifteenth | Day of March following, and then held at Cambridge.

Colophon: Boston [ ]

Collation: No title; pp. (2). L.

An Act for effectually preventing the Currency of the Bills of Credit of Connecticut, New-Hampshire and Rhode Island, within this Province. The date 1770 in the caption is an error for 1769, and in the Lenox Library copy has been corrected in manuscript. That copy is mutilated, the colophon being cut away.

1770.

[Royal Arms.] | Acts and Laws, | Passed by the Great and General Court or Assembly | of the Province of Massachusetts-Bay in New- | England, begun and held at Boston, upon Wednesday | the Thirty-first Day of May, 1769, from thence | continued by sundry Prorogations to Thursday the | fifteenth Day of March following, and then met | at Cambridge in the county of Middlesex.

Colophon: Boston: | Printed by Richard Draper, and Green & Russell, | Printers to the Government. 1770.

Collation: No title; pp. 561–568. B. H. L. P. S. W.

1770.

[Temporary.] [Royal Arms.] | Acts and Laws, | Passed by the Great and General Court or Assembly | of His Majesty's Province of the Massachusetts- | Bay, in New-England: Begun and held at Cam- | bridge, in the County of Middlesex, upon Wednes- | day the Thirtieth of May, 1770; and conti- | nued by sundry Prorogations unto Wednesday the | Twenty-sixth Day of September following, and | then met.

Colophon: Boston, | Printed by Richard Draper, and Green and Russell, | Printers to the Government. [1770.]

Collation: No title; pp. 429–450. B. H. L. P. S. W.

1770.

[Royal Arms.] | Acts and Laws, | Passed by the Great and General Court or Assembly of | the Province of the Massachusetts-Bay in New- | England: Begun and Held at Harvard-College in | Cambridge, on Wednesday the Thirtieth Day of | May, 1770, and continued by sundry Prorogations | unto Wednesday the Twenty-sixth Day of September | following, and then met.

Colophon: Boston: Printed by Richard Draper, and Green & | Russell, Printers to the Government. 1770.

Collation: No title; pp. 569–575 [1]. B. H. L. P. S. W.

1770.

[Royal Arms.] | An Act | Passed by the Great and General Court or Assembly of the Province | of the Massachusetts-Bay in New England: Begun and Held | at Harvard-College in Cambridge on Wednesday the Thirtieth | Day of May, 1770, and continued by sundry Prorogations unto | Wednesday the 26th Day of September following, and then met.

Colophon: Boston: Printed by Richard Draper, and Green & Russell, | Printers to the Government. 1770.

Collation: No title; pp. 10 [15]. S.

An Act for superceeding and repealing the two last Paragraphs in an Act made and passed . . . in the Ninth Year of his Majesty's Reign, intitled, "An Act for supplying the Treasury with the Sum of Eighty-three Thousand one Hundred and fifty-eight Pounds." The copy in the Massachusetts State Library has written in manuscript on p. 1: "Tax act 1770."

1770.

[Temporary.] [Royal Arms.] | Acts and Laws, | Passed by the Great and General Court or Assembly | of His Majesty's Province of the Massachusetts- | Bay in New-England: Begun and held at Cam- | bridge, in the County of

Middlesex, upon Wednes- | day the Thirtieth Day of May, 1770; and conti- | nued by sundry Prorogations unto Wednesday the | Third Day of April following, and then met.

Collation: No title; pp. 451–454. B. H. L. P. S. W.

1771.

[Royal Arms.] | Acts and Laws, | Passed by the Great and General Court or Assembly | of His Majesty's Province of the Massachusetts- | Bay in New-England: Begun and held at Cam- | bridge, in the County of Middlesex, upon Wednes- | day the Thirtieth Day of May, 1770; and conti- | nued by sundry Prorogations unto Wednesday the | Third Day of April following, and then met.

Colophon: Boston, N. E. Printed by Richard Dra- | per, and Green and Russell, Printers to the Go- | vernment. 1771.

Collation: No title; pp. 577–562 [589] [1].
B. H. L. P. S. W.

Pages 585 to 589 are misnumbered 558 to 562.

1771.

[Temporary.] [Royal Arms.] | Acts and Laws, | Passed by the Great and General Court or Assembly | of His Majesty's Province of the Massachusetts- | Bay, in New-England: Begun and held at Cam | bridge in the County of Middlesex, upon Wed- | nesday the twenty-ninth Day of May 1771.

Colophon: Boston; New-England: | Printed by Richard Draper, and Green & Russell, | Printers to the Government. [1771.]

Collation: No title; pp. 455–460. B. H. L. P. S. W.

Pages 457, 458, are misnumbered 557, 558.

1771.

[Temporary.] [Royal Arms.] | Acts and Laws, | Passed by the Great and General Court or Assembly | of His Majesty's

Province of the Massachusetts- | Bay, in New-England: Begun and held at Cam- | bridge in the County of Middlesex, upon Wed- | nesday the twenty-ninth Day of May 1771.

Colophon: Boston, New-England: | Printed by Richard Draper, and Green & Russell, | Printers to the Government.

Collation: No title; pp. 455–558 [458]. H. L.

This item contains Chapter i only.

1771.

[Royal Arms.] | Acts and Laws, | Passed by the Great and General Court or Assembly | of His Majesty's Province of the Massachusetts- | Bay, in New-England: Begun and held at Cam- | bridge in the County of Middlesex, upon Wed- | nesday the twenty-ninth Day of May 1771.

Collation: No title; pp. 591–599 [1]. B. H. L. P. S. W.

1771.

Province of | Massachusetts- | Bay. | [Royal Arms.] | The Honorable | Harrison Gray, Esq; | Treasurer and Receiver-General of His Majesty's said Province. | To the Select-Men or Assessors of the Town or District of —— | Greeting, &c.

Collation: No title; pp. 6. P. S.

A tax levy of £27,300 by the Provincial Treasurer, under an Act passed in 1770, the Assembly of 1771 having failed to pass a tax bill. The Massachusetts State Library copy has "Stoughton" in manuscript.

1772.

[Temporary.] [Royal Arms.] | Acts and Laws, | Passed by the Great and General Court or Assembly | of His Majesty's Province | of the Massachusetts-Bay | in New-England: Begun and held at Cambridge, in | the County of Middlesex, upon Wednesday the | twenty-ninth Day of May, 1771; and then conti- | nued by several Prorogations unto Wednesday the | eighth Day of April following, and then met.

Colophon: Printed by Richard Draper and Green & Russell, | Printers to the Government. 1772.

Collation: No title; pp. 461–466. B. H. L. P. S. W.

In some copies, p. 465 is misnumbered 46.

1772.

[Royal Arms.] |Acts and Laws, | Passed by the Great and General Court or Assembly of | His Majesty's Province of Massachusetts-Bay in | New-England: Begun and held at Cambridge | upon Wednesday the Twenty-ninth Day of May | 1771, and continued by sundry Prorogations to | Wednesday the ninth Day of April 1772, and | then met.

Colophon: Boston, New-England: | Printed by Richard Draper, and Green and Russell, | Printers to the Government. 1772.

Collation: No title; pp. 601–606. B. H. L. P. S. W.

1772.

[Temporary.] [Royal Arms.] | Acts and Laws, | Passed by the Great and General Court or Assembly | of His Majesty's Province of the Massachusetts-Bay, | in New-England: Begun and held at Cambridge, | in the County of Middlesex, upon Wednesday the | twenty-seventh Day of May 1772.

Collation: No title; pp. 467–477 [1]. B. H. L. P. S. W.

1772.

[Royal Arms.] | Acts and Laws, | Passed by the Great and General Court or Assembly | of His Majesty's Province of Massachusetts-Bay in | New-England: Begun and held at Cambridge | upon Wednesday the Twenty-seventh Day of May | 1772, and adjourned to Boston the 11th of June.

Colophon: Boston: | Printed by Richard Draper, and Green & | Russell, Printers to the Government. 1772

Collation: No title; pp. 607–623 [1]. B. H. L. P. S. W.

1772.

Province of | Massachusetts-Bay. | [Royal Arms.] | The Honorable | Harrison Gray, Esq; | Treasurer and Receiver-General of His Majesty's said Province. | To the Select-Men or Assessors of the Town or District of —— | Greeting, &c.

Colophon: Boston: Printed by Richard Draper, Printer to His Excellency the Governor, and the Honorable | His Majesty's Council, 1772.

Collation: No title; pp. 7. P. S.

A tax levy for the year 1772 similar to that of 1771. The Massachusetts State Library copy has "Stoughton" in manuscript.

1773.

[Temporary.] [Royal Arms.] | Acts and Laws, | Passed by the Great and General Court or Assem- | bly of His Majesty's Province of the Massachusetts- | Bay in New-England: Begun and held at Boston, | in the County of Suffolk upon Wednesday the | Twenty-seventh Day of May, 1772; and from | thence continued by sundry Prorogations to Wed- | nesday the Sixth Day of January following, and | then met.

Colophon: Boston, | Printed by Richard Draper, and Green and Russell, | Printers to the Government. [1773.]

Collation: No title; pp. 479–500. B. H. L. P. S. W.

1773.

[Royal Arms.] | Acts and Laws, | Passed by the Great and General Court or Assembly of His | Majesty's Province of Massachusetts-Bay in New-England: | Begun and held at Cambridge upon Wednesday the Twenty- | seventh Day of May 1772, and continued by Adjourn- | ment to Boston and several Prorogations to the 6th of January 1773, and then met.

Colophon: Boston, | Printed by Richard Draper, and Green and Russell, Printers to the | Government.

Collation: No title; pp. 625–642. B. H. L. P. S. W.

In some copies p. 630 is misnumbered 360 and p. 640 is misnumbered 140.

1773.

[Royal Arms.] | An Act | Passed by the Great and General Court or Assembly of the Province | of the Massachusetts-Bay in New-England: Begun and Held at | Boston, upon Wednesday the Twenty-sixth of May, 1773.

Colophon: Boston: Printed by Richard Draper, and Green & Russell, | Printers to the Government. 1773.

Collation: No title; pp. 9 [13]. L. P. S.

An Act for apportioning and assessing a Tax of . . . Twenty nine Thousand four hundred and fifty eight Pounds six Shillings and three Pence.

1773.

[Royal Arms.] | Acts and Laws, | Passed by the Great and General Court or Assembly | of His Majesty's Province of the Massachusetts- | Bay, in New-England: Begun and held at Boston, | upon Wednesday the twenty-sixth Day of May, | 1773.

Colophon: Boston, New-England: | Printed by Richard Draper, and Green and Russell, | Printers to the Government.

Collation: No title; pp. 643–650. B. H. L. P. S. W.

1773.

[Temporary.] [Royal Arms.] | Acts and Laws, | Passed by the Great and General Court or Assembly | of His Majesty's Province of the Massachusetts- | Bay, in New-England: Begun and held at Boston, | upon Wednesday the twenty-sixth Day of May, | 1773.

Colophon: Boston, New-England: | Printed by Richard Draper, and Green and Russell, | Printers to the Government. [1773.]

Collation: No title; pp. 501–507 [1]. B. H. L. P. S. W.

1774.

[Temporary.] [Royal Arms.] | Acts and Laws, | Passed by the Great and General Court or Assem- | bly of His Majesty's Province of the Massachusetts- | Bay, in New-England: Begun and held at Boston, | in the County of Suffolk, upon Wednesday the | Twenty-sixth Day of May, 1773; and from | thence continued by Prorogation, to Wednesday | the Twenty-sixth Day of January following, and | then met.

Colophon: Boston, | Printed by Richard Draper and Green and Russell, | Printers to the Government. [1774.]

Collation: No title; pp. 509–516. B. H. L. P. S. W.

1774.

[Royal Arms.] | Acts and Laws, | Passed by the Great and General Court or Assembly | of His Majesty's Province of the Massachusetts-Bay, | in New-England: Begun and held at Boston upon | Wednesday the twenty-sixth Day of May 1773, | and continued by sundry Prorogations to Wed-nes- | day the 26th of January following, and then met.

Colophon: Boston: Printed by Richard Draper, and Green | and Russell, Printers to the Government. 1774.

Collation: No title; pp. 651–666. B. H. L. P. S. W.

1774.

[Royal Arms.] | Acts and Laws, | Passed by the Great and General Court or Assem- | bly of the Province of Massa-chusetts-Bay, in | New-England, begun and held at Boston, upon | Wednesday the Twenty-fifth Day of May 1774, | from thence continued by Adjournment to Tues- | day the Seventh Day of June following and | then met at Salem, in the County of Essex.

Colophon: Boston: Printed by Draper, Green and Russell, | Printers to the Government. [1774.]

Collation: No title; pp. 667–670. B. H. P. S.

1774.

[Temporary.] [Royal Arms.] | Acts and Laws, | Passed by the Great and General Court or Assem- | bly of His Majesty's Province of the Massachusetts-Bay, in | New-England, begun and held at Boston, upon | Wednesday the Twenty-fifth Day of May 1774, | from thence continued by Prorogation to Tues- | day the Seventh Day of June following and | then met at Salem, in the County of Essex.

Colophon: Boston: Printed by Draper, Green and Russell, | Printers to the Government. [1774.]

Collation: No title; pp. 517–521 [1]. B. L. P. S. W.

1774.

[Royal Arms.] | An Act, | Passed by the Great and General Court or Assembly of the Province | of the Massachusetts-Bay in New-England: Begun and Held at | Boston, on Wednesday the Twenty-fifth Day of May, 1774, and | from thence continued by Adjournment to Tuesday the Seventh | Day of June following, and then met at Salem in the County of | Essex.

Colophon: Boston: Printed by Draper, Green and Russell, Printers | to the Government. [1774.]

Collation: No title; pp. 9 [13]. L. P. S.

An Act apportioning and assessing a Tax of Ten Thousand three hundred and twelve Pounds, ten shillings.

1774.

[Temporary.] [Royal Arms.] | An Act of Parliament | Passed in the Fourteenth Year of the Reign of His | Majesty King George the Third, 1774

Collation: No title; pp. 523–526. B. H. L. P. S. W.

An Act for the impartial administration of Justice in the Cases of Persons questioned for any Acts done by them in the Execution of the Law, or for the Suppression of Riots and Tumults, in the Province of the Massachusetts-Bay.

1774.

[Temporary.] [Royal Arms.] | An | Act of Parliament, | Passed in the Fourteenth Year of the Reign of His | Majesty King George the Third, 1774.

Collation: No title; pp. 527, 528. B. H. L. P. S. W.

An Act for billeting the troops in North America.

1774.

[Royal Arms.] | An Act of Parliament | Passed in the Fourteenth Year of the Reign of His | Majesty King George the Third. 1774.

Collation: No title; pp. 671–679 [1]. B. H. P. S.

An Act for the better regulating the Government of the Province of the Massachuset's Bay. At the end of the Harvard College Library copy is a manuscript index to pp. 491–642.

1775.

Acts and Laws. | Passed by the Great and General Court or Assembly of the | Colony of the Massachusetts-Bay in New-England: Be- | gun and held at Watertown, in the County of Mid- | dlesex, on Wednesday the Nineteenth Day of July, Anno | Domini, 1775.

Colophon: Watertown, New-England: | Printed by Benjamin Edes, Printer to the Honorable | Council and Honorable House of Representatives. | M,DCC,LXXV.

Collation: No title; pp. 1–7 [1]. B. H. L. N. S. W.

1775.

Acts and Laws | Passed by the Great and General Court or Assembly of the | Colony of the Massachusetts-Bay in New-England: Be- | gun | and held at Watertown, in the County of Middlesex, | on Wednesday the Nineteenth Day of July, Anno Do- | mini, 1775: And from thence continued by Adjourn- | ment to Wednesday the | Twentieth Day of September | following, and then met.

Colophon: Watertown: New-England. | Printed by Benjamin Edes, Printer to the Honorable Council, | and Honorable House of Representatives. | M,DCC,LXXV.

Collation: No title; pp. 9–13 [1]. B. H. L. N. S. W.

The Lenox Library copy lacks pp. 9–12.

1775.

An Act | Passed by the Great and General Court or Assembly of the Colony of the Massachu- | setts-Bay, in New-England: Begun and held at Watertown, in the County of | Middlesex, on Wednesday the Nineteenth Day of July 1775, and from thence con- | tinued by Adjournment to Wednesday the Twentieth Day of September follow- | ing, and then met.

Colophon: Watertown, New England: | Printed by Benjamin Edes, Printer to the Honorable Council, and Honorable | House of Representatives. M,DCC,LXXV.

Collation; No title; pp. 9 [1]. P. S.

An Act apportioning and assessing a Tax of Forty-six Thousand Pounds.

1776.

Acts and Laws, | Passed by the Great and General Court or Assembly of the | Colony of the Massachusetts-Bay in New England: Be- | gun and held at Watertown, in the County of Middle- |sex, on Wednesday the Nineteenth Day of July, Anno Domini, 1775. And from thence continued by

Adjourn- | ments to Wednesday the Twenty-ninth Day of November | following and then met.

Colophon: Watertown: | Printed by Benjamin Edes, Printer to the Honorable | Council, and Honorable House of Represen- | tatives. 1776.

Collation: No title; pp. 15–59. B. H. L. N. S. W.

The Boston Public Library copy has pp. 55–58 torn. The Harvard College Library copy lacks pp. 57, 58. The Lenox Library copy lacks pp. 15–22. The headline on p. 31 reads: "In the Sixteenth Year of the Reign of George the Third, King, &c. 1776." The headline on p. 32 reads: "1776. In the Year of Our Lord, One Thousand seven Hundred and Seventy-six."

1776.

Acts and Laws, | Passed by the Great and General Court or Assembly of the | Colony of the Massachusetts-Bay in New-England: Be- | gun and held at Watertown, in the County of Middlesex, | on Wednesday the Twenty-ninth of May, in the | Year of our Lord, 1776.

Colophon: Watertown: New-England. | Printed by Benjamin Edes, Printer to the Honorable | Council, and Honorable House of Representatives. | M,DCC,LXXVI.

Collation: No title; pp. 61–59 [69] [1]. B. H. L. N. S. W.

Page 69 is misnumbered 59. The Boston Public Library copy has p. 69 mutilated.

1776.

Resolves | of the | General Assembly | of the | Colony | of | Massachusetts-Bay, | Begun and held at Watertown, in the County of | Middlesex, on Wednesday the 29th Day of May, | being the last Wednesday in said Month, Anno | Domini, 1776.

Collation: Title, 1 leaf; Resolves, pp. 3–59 [1]. H. L. S.

The Harvard College Library copy lacks Title.

REPRINTS OF LEGAL CLASSICS PUBLISHED BY THE LAWBOOK EXCHANGE, LTD.

LEGAL BIBLIOGRAPHY

Benedict, Russell. *Acts and Laws of the Thirteen Original Colonies and States: Constituting the extraordinary collection of Hon. Russell Benedict.* New York: American Art Association, 1922. [272]pp. Reprinted 1998 The Lawbook Exchange, Ltd. LC 98-20196 ISBN 1-886363-56-0. Cloth. $85.

* An indispensable complement to *The Charlemagne Tower Collection of Colonial Laws*, this catalogue is still very useful and provides an invaluable resource for the scholar or collector of early Americana.The collection of Hon. Russell Benedict included rare titles relating to acts and laws of the thirteen original colonies and states. Very rich in detail, this catalogue of 479 items includes meticulous collation and issue descriptions, annotations, references and location information, as well as reproductions of selected title pages. These items were sold at an unrestricted public sale on February 27, 1922 under the management of The American Art Association, New York.

[Blackstone, William]. Eller, Catherine Spicer. *The William Blackstone Collection in the Yale Law Library. A Bibliographical Catalogue.* New Haven: Yale University Press, 1938. xvii, 113 pp. Reprinted 1993 by The Lawbook Exchange, Ltd. LCCN 99-38826. ISBN 0-9630106-5-4. Cloth. $50.

* The definitive Blackstone bibliography. Reprint of the first and only edition (1938). This catalogue contains all the printed material which was collated by the compiler and was primarily a description of books owned by the Yale Law Library and Yale University Library, but also includes information concerning other editions known to exist. Includes English, American, Irish and foreign editions of the *Commentaries* as well as his other works, works founded on the *Commentaries* and biography and criticism.

DePuy, Henry F. *A Bibliography of the English Colonial Treaties with the American Indians.* New York: the Lenox Club, 1917. [108] pp. Reprinted 2001 by The Lawbook Exchange, Ltd. ISBN 1-58477-163-1. Cloth. $50.

* Many of the records of the various treaties with the Indians exist only in manuscript. This bibliography locates and describes fifty treaties that were separately printed in small print quantities and thus are exceedingly rare. For each treaty De Puy provides full collation, a brief synopsis of the contents, an illustration, and the location of copies in principal libraries and private collections. Besterman, *A World Bibliography of Bibliographies* 352.

Ford, Worthington Chauncey and Albert Matthews. *A Bibliography of the Laws of the Massachusetts Bay 1641-1776.* Reprinted from the Publications of The Colonial Society of Massachusetts Vol. IV. Cambridge: Privately Printed, 1907. vi, 186 pp. Reprint available 2003 by The Lawbook Exchange, Ltd. ISBN 1-58477-284-0. Cloth. $85.
* Lists the acts and laws of Massachusetts as published from 1641-1776, with collation, locations and relevant notes. Ford was the brother of the historian Paul Leicester Ford. Marke, *A Catalogue of the Law Collection at New York University* (1953) 1199.

Friend, Willam L. *Anglo-American Legal Bibliographies. An Annotated Guide.* Washington, D.C.: United States Government Printing Office, 1944. xii, 166 pp. Reprinted 1996 by The Lawbook Exchange, Ltd. LCCN 96-11002. ISBN 1-886363-21-8. Cloth. $65. * This extensively annotated bibliography provides a complete bibliographical analysis of 298 significant works in Anglo-American legal literature. Friend has omitted "nothing of legal bibliographical importance" in his descriptions and has included the Library of Congress catalogue entry and number for each title. Entries are arranged in alphabetical order by author, followed by a comprehensive index. Friend introduces his study with a lengthy historical survey of the important developments in legal bibliography.

James, Eldon Revare. *A List of Legal Treatises Printed in the British Colonies and the American States Before 1801.* Cambridge, Mass.: Harvard University Press, 1934. 52 pp. Reprinted 2002 by The Lawbook Exchange, Ltd. ISBN 1-58477-143-7. Cloth. $50.
* A bibliography of items published in Britain and the United States between 1687-1800, organized by date, with complete title page transcriptions. During these years most law books were printed for the benefit of the officer or layman who was called upon to act in a legal capacity. Therefore legal manuals, formbooks, pocket-books, young clerk's *vade mecums*, justice of the peace manuals, the *Conductor Generalis* and the like provided the legal sources of the time. This bibliography contains occasional annotations regarding the various printings. Originally published in *Harvard Legal Essays.*

Marke, Julius J., editor. *A Catalogue of the Law Collection at New York University With Selected Annotations.* New York: The Law Center of New York University, 1953. xxxi, 1372 pp. Reprinted 1999 by The Lawbook Exchange, Ltd. LCCN 99-19939. ISBN 1-886363-91-9. Cloth. $185.
* Reprint of the massive, well-annotated catalogue compiled by the librarian of the School of Law at New York University. Classifies approximately 15,000 works excluding foreign law, by Sources of the Law, History of Law and its Institutions, Public and Private Law, Comparative Law, Jurisprudence and Philosophy of Law, Political and Economic Theory, Trials, Biography, Law and Literature, Periodicals and Serials, and Reference Material. With a thorough subject and author index. This reference volume will be of continuous value to the legal scholar and bibliographer, due not only to the works included but to the

authoritative annotations, often citing more than one source. Besterman, *A World Bibliography of Bibliographies* 3461.

[Marshall, John]. Servies, James Albert. *A Bibliography of John Marshall.* Washington: United States Commission for the Celebration of the Two Hundredth Anniversary of the Birth of John Marshall, 1956. xix, 182 pp. Reprinted 2000 by The Lawbook Exchange, Ltd. LCCN 99-088239. ISBN 1-58477-083-X. Cloth. $65.
* Compiled by the reference librarian of the College of William and Mary as an official publication of the United States Commission for the bicentennial of Marshall's birth, this bibliography includes all of Marshall's known published documents arranged by year of composition, and selected, annotated references to printed materials about Marshall.

Maxwell, W. Harold and C.R. Brown. *A Complete List of British and Colonial Law Reports and Legal Periodicals. Arranged in Alphabetical and in Chronological Order with Bibliographical Notes.* **[With]:** *Check List of Canadian and Newfoundland Statutes.*[Third Edition]. Toronto: The Carswell Company, Limited, 1937. viii, 141, 49 pp. Reprinted 1995 by The Lawbook Exchange, Ltd. LCCN 96-14504. ISBN 1-886363-11-0. Cloth. $70.
* This comprehensive guide includes every known edition of every British or Colonial law report (except American reprints). This edition also includes a list of the various territories in the British Empire which had issued printed legislation. Librarians and scholars will find this a particularly useful checklist, with notes that supplement Soule's earlier *Lawyer's Reference Manual.*

Schroeder, Theodore. *Free Speech Bibliography Including Every Discovered Attitude Toward the Problem Covering Every Method of Transmitting Ideas and Abridging Their Promulgation upon Every Subject-Matter.* New York: The H.W. Wilson Company, 1922. [vii], 247 pp. Reprinted 2001 by The Lawbook Exchange, Ltd. LCCN 99-049361. ISBN 1-58477-053-8. Cloth. $85.
* Annotated bibliography organized by subject. General categories include works issued before 1800, general discussions, alien and sedition laws of 1768, economic motive, personal motive, religious motive, sedition, sex motive, war motive, and suppressed publications. Sub-categories include slavery, chattel, anarchists, trials, church and state, heresy, labor unionists, art, theater. With a thorough author index. Schroeder [1864-1953] was a founding member of the Free Speech League.

[Worrall, John and Edward Brooke]. *Bibliotheca Legum Angliae. Or, a Catalogue of the Common and Statute Law Books of This Realm, and Some Others Relating Thereto: Giving an Account of Their Several Editions, Ancient Printers, Dates, and Prices, and Wherein They Differ. [With a Supplement to 1800]. Part I Compiled by John Worrall, Part II and Supplement Compiled by Edward Brooke. Parts I, II and Supplement bound in one volume.* London: Printed for Edward Brooke, 1788-1800. [15], 272, [26]; viii, 40, 49-255, [1]; [3], 45, [2] pp. 1788-1800. Reprinted

1997 by The Lawbook Exchange, Ltd. LCCN 97-12962. ISBN 1-886363-29-3. Cloth. $110.

* First annotated English legal bibliography. John Worrall, believed to be the first law bookseller, issued the first edition in 1732, and published numerous editions during his lifetime. Part I is organizedby topic and then alphabetically. Topics include abridgments, indexes, tables; civil, ecclesiastical, and universal law; common law, crown law; constitution, crown and Parliament; courts; dictionaries; trade, navigation; reports; statutes; and Irish and Scottish law books. Part II is prefaced by a historical account of English legal literature from the earliest times to the reign of George III.

This edition consists of a reprint of Parts I and II of the 1788 edition, and includes the uncommon supplement published in 1800. This edition continues Worrall's experiment begun in the 1782 edition of including observations by learned law writers in the annotation to some entries. This last development marked a positive step of the bare Bassett style of catalogue, which Worrall had originally followed and which was to influence future bibliographies. With an index to each Part. An important, indispensable reference.